Management Consultants' Acceptance of Internet Technology

An Empirical Study of the Determinants of Web Analytics Technology Acceptance

Kennedy K Amofa PhD.

Lulu Publishing Services rev. date: 08/10/2016

Contents

List of Tables

List of Figures

I would like first of all to dedicate this work to the Almighty God for the strength and the grace to enable me to complete this difficult journey. I want to dedicate this work to the memory of my father, Samuel Amofa (Yaw Atta), who initiated this great vision for me as his first son; my mother, Comfort Boakye (Akosua Boatemaa); and my auntie, Theresa Aning (Adwoa Sewaa), who laid the foundation of my education, both in Ghana and in the United States. I equally want to dedicate this work to my dear wife, Rosemary, who inspired and encouraged me throughout this long journey, and to my three kids, Amanda, Theresa, and Samuel, who were with me all the time and were all a great source of encouragement to get this project done.

Background

The versatility and the increased capability of the Internet as part of organizational information technology (IT) infrastructure has led to the emerging of new technologies, including web analytics technology (WAT), to help aggregate and integrate online user behavior data for management operations and strategic planning. The research study developed a model based on unified theory of acceptance use of technology (UTAUT) premises to provide empirical evidence to support management consultants' acceptance of WAT. The study explored quantitative research methodology and online survey technique that involved 270 management consultants. The results of the study showed that there is a positive correlation among the determinants including effort expectations, performance expectation, social influence, facilitating conditions, and behavioral intentions. The study established that performance expectancy, effort expectancy, social influence, and facilitating conditions can predict 62 percent of the behavior intention of management consultants to accept WAT. The study underscored the impacts of the research findings on the organizational strategic IT management, management consulting industry, IT solutions vendors, and academia on the phenomenon of technology acceptance in organizational settings. The research study furnished the theoretical framework and recommendations for future research studies to further investigate WAT acceptance and usage.

CHAPTER 1

Introduction

The twenty-first-century business environment is marked with rapid technological advancement and keen global competition. The increasing volatility and uncertainty looming over the business environment have compelled business leaders to invest in advanced technology to enhance productivity and performance (Melville, Kraemer, and Gurbaxani 2004; Nakata, Zhu, and Kraimer 2008). In the midst of a difficult global business environment, management consultants' services are critical for supporting organizations to create value and to maintain sustainable growth. Over time, the management consulting industry has provided important services to enhance business operations and management in the global marketplace (Kitay and Wright 2003; Turner 1982).

The evolution of the Internet has helped to transform business operations and management over time to meet the dynamic demands and expectations of the global marketplace (Angehrn 1997). Web analytics technology (WAT) generates firsthand online customer behavior data to supplement existing data for strategic planning and decision-making processes (Sen, Dacin, and Pattichis 2006). Research studies done on WAT are limited and fragmented; it appears that there are no comprehensive research studies done to examine the reasons why potential users of WAT accept or reject this new technology.

This research study explores the unified theory of acceptance use of technology (UTAUT) as a theoretical base to investigate the important drivers of WAT acceptance in the context of management consulting. Previous studies on technology acceptance enable researchers in the field of information systems (IS), along with other fields of academic study, to identify specific trends of technology acceptance through the study of external variables including belief, behavioral intentions, and actual usage (Lee, Kozar, and Larsen 2003).

Researchers across various geographical settings have used the UTAUT model from different conceptual and theoretical perspectives based on the recommendations of Vankatesh et al. (2003) to replicate the model in different contexts to test its validity and reliability. This investigation of management consultant acceptance of WAT might add to the body of knowledge in both IS literature and organizational management.

Background of the Study

Considering that the global market structure has become more and more complex over the past decade and that competition is keen and consumer behavior unpredictable, organizational leaders are increasingly dependent on the external services of management consultants to sustain a reliable and efficient value chain (Fincham 1999; Amit and Zott 2001). Consulting firms provide essential services to organizations in various industries while maintaining sustainable relationships with clients. These efforts, along with outstanding leadership expectations and management practices in the global market, have a great impact on organizational growth (Gable 1996; Sturdy 1997; Weiss, H 2004). Consulting firms provide business leaders with visionary prospects to explore business opportunities in the global marketplace.

The management consulting industry has evolved over the years, and many consulting firms have recorded higher margins due to this remarkable growth; thus, many academic researchers and practitioners have developed a keen interest in critical analyses of the consulting process and practice (Schein 1969; Stumpf and Tymon 2001; Weiss, A 2004). The results of the initiatives of most large organizations over the last two decades to implement major structural changes have propelled the need for contracted external consultant services to assist with the change-management process. The management consulting industry continues to provide essential services to organizations involving complex business structures and issues as a result of technology and globalization (Menon and Pfeffer 2003).

The role of management consultants varies, depending on the area of focus or the specialization, but their major roles are as coaches, expert advisors, partners, providers, implementers, organizational developers, and those of other market niches (McLarty and Robinson 1998). Consultants aid other processes, which might include marketing, technology, visioning, and brand-identity investment. The nature and scope of the management consultant contract determine assigned roles and expectations.

The larger organizations involve variations of job roles and assignments, depending on individual experience and expertise, but the small consulting firms often specialize in niche markets that demand unique skills and expertise (Hislop 2002).

Because both large and small consulting firms have varied roles when it comes to the question of how best to serve their clients, four dominant roles serve to identify the kind of services that management consultants provide to their prospective clients. These roles involve consultants as advisers, implementers, providers, and partners (Stumpf 1999).

In difficult economic downturns, organizational leaders seek the expert advice of management consultants to complement the efforts of internal management resources in resolving complex issues, as well as getting a broader perspective and objective appraisal of any given business issues. The situation is similar as organizations attain organic growth and explore global opportunities—they still rely on external consultants to make well-informed decisions (Graubner and Richter 2003). Consultants in advisor roles tend to establish sustainable relationships with clients that extend beyond the traditional expectations of helping organizations to overcome specific challenges, but they also build social ties and mutual relationships. These long-term partnerships are essential for continuous engagement and repeat business for the consultants to play a proactive role in the organization (Anand, Glick, and Manz 2002).

Although the management consulting industry has contributed to the development of business models and innovative organizational management concepts and practices, almost no significant research studies have been done that involve the impact of technology on management consultants. Greiner and Poulfelt (2010) evaluated this situation: "Information technology is a major force impacting the development of the consulting business. Surprisingly, we cannot find a single research study on the impact and implications of technology on management consulting" (p. 462). The new wave of digitization inherent on the web calls for more empirical and scientific research studies to enhance understanding of the impacts of technology on the consulting industry and how this expertise and knowledge can be used to advise leaders in other organizations. The research study on management consultants' acceptance of WAT might provide important insight into better understanding technology acceptance in the management consulting industry and offer new ways to enhance technology acceptance.

The Internet revolution over the last two decades has prompted a widespread proliferation of software companies that provide technical support and packaged IT solutions to organizations. Kim, Park, and Koh (2010) considered web analytics services as an emerging rapidly growing business sector of software companies and other Internet businesses that facilitate organizations to build and sustain online business models and strategies. Web analytics businesses offer important services to business partners to enable them to create web analytic reports for strategic planning and the decision-making process. Hopkins reported that for the past decade, senior executives expect the IT management team to look beyond the traditional function of IT to find analytics solutions (2011). Such solutions can create a competitive advantage and guide the strategic decision-making process.

Organizational leadership teams continue to explore the capabilities of web analytics to identify and leverage online data-driven insights for enhancing decision-making processes and increasing performance (Bose 2009). Organizations like eBay, Google, Amazon, and IBM use this online business strategy and have taken the initiative to collect and analyze online data to understand their customers' online activities for policy development and implementation (Hamm 2009; Goldsborough 2005; Ogle 2010; Schaupp 2010). WAT enables organizational management to build sustainable online business models.

The Internet has become a medium of communication that serves as the hub for systematic exploration of large-scale digital data. With increasing Internet capabilities and the growth of e-business, the need to evaluate commercial websites has gained more attention (Kent, Carr, Husted, and Pop 2011).The Internet provides a universal platform for WAT in the form of software and application programs to aggregate, query, and analyze online digital data (Welling and White 2006; Wittmann 2009). The actual task is not just amassing data from the business website, but also includes the process of evaluating the massive data to create more complicated business value. Researchers including Phippen, Sheppard, and Furnell (2004) observed that the traditional methods used to evaluate web usage in the form of web logs data lack the needed capabilities and the richness to support decision-making processes. WAT can be easily integrated into the existing information technology (IT) infrastructure to provide value for the organization.

Organizational websites function as an important interface between the firm and the outside world to enhance effective communication between organizations and their customers (Heldal, Sjovold, and Heldal 2004). WAT works by evaluating the clicks and keystrokes of customers' website activities as a web server records the gathered data (Nstase and Dragos 2010). The data is then processed to provide strategic insights to assist managerial decision-making and operational management. Several research studies support the claim that WAT creates a unique platform to enhance business intelligence (Phippen 2004; Ranjit 2009; Reeser and Hariharan 2002). WAT, in the form of predictive analytics including data mining and text mining, accounts for rich customer data based on web activities. Peterson (2009) argued that the successful implementation of WAT as an IT strategy requires the involvement of senior management and a team of analysts coordinating with other organizational employees to use web data to study market segments, product design, and new market opportunities.

The websites that use WAT serve as the hub for information processing and sharing to gain business insights. Zhang and Segal (2008) evaluated three different types of web mining: web content mining, web usage mining, and web structure mining, which together provide a traffic measurement that can be used in addition to other tools that include short quantitative surveys, databases, and RSS feeds from other dominant websites, including social media. WAT provides the capability and the options to prioritize needed speed, flexibility, and visualized reporting styles, such as dashboards (Wilson 2010).

Rapoza (2010) explained the current overview of WAT, which comes in the form of different analytics packages that can analyze data from varied sources, including mobile data, e-mail campaigns, data from cloud-based services, and data in the form of feeds from external sites, including news websites and social networks.

WAT provides essential insights to direct, optimize, and automate the decision-making process to achieve organizational goals. Web-mining technologies, including text and data mining, provide a great opportunity to coordinate other advanced analytics with the existing data warehouse. Phippen et al.'s research studies exhibit the capability of web analytics to measure the success of web sites and to improve their performance in both business-to-consumer (B2C) and business-to-business (B2B) applications (2004). To customize website operations to meet the needs of customers and to provide solutions to encountered issues, WAT enables organizational leaders to use online data (Plaza, 2009; Chatterjee and Jana, 2004). WAT also provides necessary strategic insights so that organizations can build sustainable online business models to attain efficiency and organic growth and create shareholder value (Treiblmaier, 2007). Increased computing power, the continuous decline in cost for data storage, and increasingly efficient database systems have enabled organizations to collect, store, and process higher amounts of data. WAT furnishes clickstream data that captures important information to measure website performance (Goldman, 2007; Liberatore and Luo, 2010). Web analytics software can aid in analyzing the captured information in the form of clickstream data to understand website usage and navigation patterns of visitors and to provide B2B marketing managers with an insightful mechanism for improving website performance (Kohavi, Rothleder, and Simoudis, 2002). Research studies purport that WAT can improve operational efficiency through data mining and statistical models to provide near real-time snapshots of key performance indicators (KPI) to advise process-change management (Omidvar, Mirabi, and Shokry, 2011).

Corporate websites serve as information hubs for business activities, and WAT delivers rich online data to sustain value-chain management sourced from customer online activities and other business partners to assist organizations to improve customer satisfaction, retention, and partnerships (Miranda and Bañegil, 2004; Nauck, Azvine, and Ho, 2003). Research studies done in the context of libraries extend the understanding of WAT and how administrators can use acquired data about the user's online behavior to provide important services to these customers (Black, 2009; Crawford and Fang, 2008; Farney, 2011; Marek, 2011; Price and Trainor, 2010). Even though WAT in its infancy stage, both large and small businesses are exploring new ways to use it to improve their business operations.

Conversely, Paul and Erdelez highlighted a limitation of WAT in that it does not account for the reasons behind online customer behavior, leaving room for speculative information that can be misleading under certain circumstances (2009). Given all the research studies on how WAT can be an essential tool for business leaders and management teams to create value to meet business expectations, little is known about the reasons why they have accepted or rejected this technology. Furthermore, there are no significant research studies on WAT adoption in the context of the management consulting industry; therefore, the researcher explored the determinants of WAT adoption by using the UTUAT model presented by Venkatesh et al. (2003).

Statement of the Problem

In the twenty-first century global economy, the impact of rapid technological advancement has strongly motivated organizational leaders to seek innovative technologies to create, manage, and share vital information to attain a competitive edge. Researchers and practitioners have identified WAT as one of the innovative technologies that can use advanced algorithms to aggregate, analyze, and integrate customer online behavior data for strategic planning and operational management, yet it has not been used widely.

It is unclear why senior managers are not using WAT, despite its numerous advantages for evidence-based decision-making and strategic planning. There is a knowledge gap in IS literature on a comprehensive study on WAT acceptance, for related research studies are limited and scanty. Given that the UTAUT model by Venkatesh et al. (2003) has accounted for up to 70 percent accuracy in predicting user acceptance of information technology innovations, this model is used in this study to investigate the important drivers of management consultant acceptance of WAT.

Purpose of the Study

The main objective of the study is to examine how management consultants perceive WAT. In this study, empirical methods were used to identify the significant determinants of WAT acceptance by management consultants and measure the relationship among the determinants. The effects of the moderating factors, including age, gender, and experience, were ascertained on the main constructs. The UTAUT model was validated through testing of the main constructs in different contexts, with the management consulting industry deviating from the customary usage of students as the sample population. The study might contribute to the literature on management consulting by addressing the issue of the impact of technological advancement on the management consultant industry. Through this study, new streams of research on related topics of technology acceptance might be opened. The intent of the researcher was to find significant determinants of WAT acceptance to provide recourse for change management in fully embracing an evidence-based decision-making process.

Rationale

The computing environment is constantly changing, and Internet technologies are making the web more essential for global business operations. Understanding the important drivers behind WAT can help management team members augment their available information resources with online user behavior data and RSS feeds from other websites, including social media, for strategic decision making. Along with rising web usage and the insurgence of new e-business initiatives, the study of management consultant acceptance of web analytics might open more research streams on how technology can shape the management consultant industry and other businesses that use web analytics.

Voluminous data from multiple sources take the form of both structured and unstructured data that are sometimes in real-time, requiring WAT to generate informed and evidence-based decisions. This study adds to IS literature on the technology acceptance model specifically applied to WAT acceptance. The results of this research study could be used to predict potential user acceptance and WAT practices for the development and implementation of IS policies in organizations.

Research Questions

1. The main objective of this study was to provide empirical evidence to substantiate claims for WAT. To guide the study, the following research questions were developed:
2. What are the significant determinants of management consultant acceptance of WAT?
3. To what extent do the main UTAUT variables (performance expectancy, effort expectancy, social influence, and facilitating conditions) influence management consultant intentions to accept WAT?

To what extent do the moderating factors (gender, age, and experience) impact the four determinants (performance expectancy, effort expectancy, social influence, and facilitating conditions)?

The hypotheses are stated as follows:

$H1_A$: Performance expectancy will positively affect behavioral intention to accept WAT.

$H1_0$: Performance expectancy will negatively affect behavioral intention to accept WAT.

$H2_A$: Effort expectancy will positively affect behavioral intention to accept WAT.

$H2_0$: Effort expectancy will negatively affect behavioral intention to accept WAT.

$H3_A$: Social influence will positively affect behavioral intention to accept WAT. $H3_0$: Social influence will negatively affect behavioral intention to accept WAT. $H4_A$: Facilitating conditions will positively affect behavioral intentions to accept WAT.

$H4_0$: Facilitating conditions will negatively affect behavioral intentions to accept WAT.

$H5_A$: Gender will affect behavioral intention to accept WAT (positively for men and negatively for women).

$H5_0$: Gender will not affect behavioral intention to accept WAT (positively for men, negatively for women).

$H6_A$: Age will positively affect behavioral intention to accept WAT.

$H6_0$: Age will negatively affect behavioral intention to accept WAT.

$H7_A$: Experience will positively affect behavioral intention to accept WAT. $H7_0$: Experience will negatively affect behavioral intention to accept WAT.

Significance of the Study

The study adds to IS literature in its exploration of the important determinants of WAT and how the findings might extend understanding of WAT in business settings. From an organizational management perspective, this study contributes to the body of literature on evidence-based management by identifying significant drivers of WAT. WAT is a valuable resource for enhancing change management to integrate the concept of analytics to strategic decision-making processes and other management operations. The research study contributes to other studies in the management consulting industry that analyze the phenomenon of technological impacts on the industry.

Management consultants and senior managers can benefit from the insights gained from the important predictors of WAT and how it can be used as a business tool to enhance evidence-based decisions. Web analytics service providers and other IT vendor companies can benefit from knowing the relationship of the determinants of WAT acceptance for successful organizational implementation. The research study on WAT might provide essential information about customer online user behavior to enable website developers and website content managers to make their sites more functional to meet potential user expectations.

Definition of Terms

Web Analytics Technology (WAT): An Internet-embedded technology that monitors and reports website usage to provide website users' online activities data.

Enterprise Resource Planning System (ERP): A comprehensive software package that integrates business processes and functions into a holistic IT infrastructure (Klaus, Rosemann, and Gable, 2000).

Online Analytical Processing (OLAP): A software package that provides multidimensional analysis of data stored in the database to all the business functions of an organization, either through an intranet or the Internet.

Technology Acceptance Model (TAM): A model developed originally by Davis (1986) to explain the concept of individual technology adoption behavior.

Unified Theory of Acceptance Use of Technology (UTAUT): A model developed by Venkatesh et al. (2003) to explain user technology acceptance and usage with the integration of eight different technology adoption models.

Assumptions and Limitations

In this study, the researcher took into consideration certain assumptions and limitations due to time constraints, a limited budget, and the availability of data. The researcher assumed that all participants have adequate knowledge of WAT and that they are able to answer the questionnaires to the best of their knowledge. In using online survey techniques, the participants' responses are limited by their willingness to be honest in self-reporting and by their ability to recollect events reliably.

Because WAT is still in its seminal stages and is a new technology with low capability awareness, the likelihood exists that possible biases can be present. The study is a cross-sectional one that makes use of convenient samples geographically limited to the United States. However, user perception and attitude regarding a phenomenon can change over time (Venkatesh et al., 2003). Moreover, to attain generalizability, it is recommended that this study be replicated using a longitudinal research methodology and, most importantly, with a different population, or with the same population in a different geographical area.

Nature of the Study

The study builds on the conceptual framework of UTAUT as defined by Venkatesh et al. (2003). In this research study, management consultant's behavioral intentions to accept WAT were measured. The research design consisted of a quantitative method using an online survey research technique. Prior research studies that employed the UTAUT model provided empirical evidence that the model tends to be an accurate predictor of new technologies (Anderson, Schwager, and Kerns, 2006; Minishi-Majanja and Dulle, 2011; Venkatesh et al., 2003). Because WAT is new technology, the UTAUT model is comprehensive and provides a broad spectrum for explaining the determinants of WAT.

The objective of the research model was, first, to investigate the relationship between the direct determinant as the behavioral intention (BI) and the four main UTAUT variables (performance expectancy, effort expectancy, social influence, and facilitating conditions). Second, the model ascertained the effect of the moderating factors (gender, age, and experience) on the three determinants (performance expectancy, effort expectancy, and social influence). The fourth moderation factor of voluntariness was eliminated, for the research focused mainly on a mandatory environment. The research model equally identified the significant drivers of WAT acceptance. This research study based on the UTAUT model is presented in Figure 1.

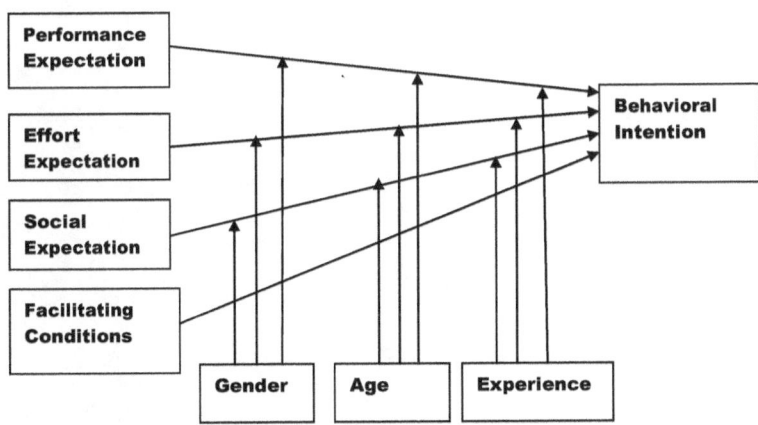

Figure 1. Moderating factors and the four determinants. Adapted from a study of UTAUT by Venkatesh et al. (2003)

Organization of the Remainder of the Study

In this chapter, the research objectives and what was intended to be accomplished were outlined, and the way in which the study will contribute to IS literature on the area of technology adoption was discussed. Chapter 2 presents literature on individual technology and Internet adoption. The evaluation of research studies on WAT and the theoretical framework based on the UTAUT model initiate the investigation into the important determinants of WAT adoption. In Chapter 3, the methodology and the scientific instruments used for the research study is presented. The focus in Chapter 4 is on the analysis of the data collected for the research process. In Chapter 5 are discussions about the findings that conclude the research studies, along with the recommendations and limitations of the study.

CHAPTER 2

Literature Review

To extend understanding of the factors contributing to the sustained usage of IS, researchers have developed several technology acceptance models, including the UTAUT. The literature review presents an overview of technology acceptance models as they relate to the UTAUT model for the present study. According to Szajna (1996), the UTAUT model creates a unified platform that consists of multiple IS technology models. Its purpose is to explain the significant determinants of new technologies that make it most suitable for evaluating management consultant acceptance of WAT. This chapter examines research studies on individual technology acceptance, research framework based on the UTAUT model, other relevant research studies done using the UTAUT model, and how the UTAUT model is appropriate to examine management consultants' acceptance of WAT.

Individual Technology Acceptance

For the past few decades, researchers and practitioners have used different models and theoretical frameworks to explain individual technology acceptance and usage in a different given context (Venkatesh et al., 2003). Prior research studies on technology acceptance focus on the constructs of user satisfaction and attitude and how they influence individual technology acceptance. The introduction of the original Technology Acceptance

Model (TAM) developed by Davis (1989) and Davis, Bagozzi, and Warshaw (1989) indicated that the two constructs of *perceived ease* and *perceived importance* have a significant influence when it comes to questioning the intentions of evaluating user acceptance of a given IS.

According to Venkatesh et al. (2007), the robustness and reliability of the scales of the TAM helped in the facilitation of several studies to replicate the model in diverse scientific research endeavors for attaining generalizability. In more than 1,000 studies, researchers have cited the TAM as the theoretical framework in both IS and other fields of study, including health and behavioral sciences (Venkatesh et al., 2007). Venkatesh, Brown, Maruping, and Bala (2008) observed that the TAM has been the prevailing model for examining individual technology acceptance as more researchers use the model as the foundation for building their theoretical framework.

In this information age, technology has enhanced effective communication and collaboration in all sectors and fields of study. The noticeable trend in IS literature reveals that researchers have successfully combined theories that originated from diverse fields of study, including psychology, sociology, and medical sciences, to examine the underlying determinants of technology acceptance and usage at the workplace (Davis, 1989; Davis et al., 1989; Venkatesh et al., 2003). Researchers in these fields of study have tested the models of technology acceptance to determine the significant factors that influence such acceptance.

The constructs of individual user belief and attitude introduced by Fishbein and Ajzen (1975) have been fundamental in most of the research studies on technology acceptance. The study of the constructs of beliefs and attitudes has provided researchers with perspectives to understand individual behavioral intentions to use IS. The constructs of beliefs and attitudes of users toward technology help to determine individual technology acceptance and new ways of predicting actual usage (Venkatesh and Davis, 2000).

Given that technology has become an integral part of organizational structure, IS studies that pertain to the organizational settings explored various aspects of how technology fit in the entire organizational structure as a task-technology fit (Leonard-Barton and Deschamps, 1988; Goodhue and Thompson, 1995; Spitler, 2005; Harun, 2002). Using technology as a tool to enhance productivity and performance has become eminent in a technology-driven economy. Consequently, research studies

done in the field of IS have established several factors that have a significant influence on user acceptance of technology (Agarwal and Prasad, 1997; Ajzen, 1991; Compeau and Higgins, 1995; Davis, 1989; Taylor and Todd, 1995; Venkatesh and Davis, 2000).

Another stream of IS research studies on technology acceptance focused on the importance factors that led to the successful implementation of IS policies in organizations (Hong and Kim, 2002; Sharma and Yetton, 2003; Tyran and George, 1993). With identified numerous challenges of IS policies' development and implementation, these research studies provide important insights to understand the technology acceptance process in organizations. With the given circumstances that organizational leaders consider IT as critical to meeting the expectation of the global market, several research studies have been done to examine the factors that significantly impact individual technology acceptance and usage at the workplace (Venkatesh et al., 2003; Davis, 1989; Davis et al., 1989).

Certain IS researchers differentiated between technology acceptance in a production-based environment termed as utilitarian and entertainment-oriented as hedonic. Ja-Chul Fan, Suh, and Sang-Chul (2010) conducted research studies using samples of two different user groups, students and employees, to differentiate between the two as utilitarian and hedonic. The results indicated that employees are significantly affected by utilitarian usefulness, whereas the students are mostly affected by hedonic usefulness. The implications of the research study of Ja-Chul et al. (2010) supported previous research studies that proposed that there is the tendency of a utilitarian system to enhance users' ability to increase task performance, and the hedonic system furnishes pleasure to the user (Crowley, Spangenberg, and Hughes, 1992; Heijden, 2004).

Literature on technology acceptance reveals two important environmental settings as the voluntary and the mandatory that have significant impact on individual technology acceptance. Chan et al. (2010) indicated that the results of prior research studies done in the context of mandatory environment and then replicated in a mandatory use context still lack clarity. To explain further, researchers like Brown et al. (2002) proposed that both mandatory and voluntary research environments might indicate different underlying relationships regarding the traditional technology acceptance model. Specifically, research studies show that moderating factors like voluntary use can have significant effects on the main determinants of behavioral intention to accept a given system (Venkatesh et al., 2003). On the contrary, certain IS researchers have found that besides behavioral intention, user satisfaction tends to be an appropriate dependent construct in mandatory environments for technology acceptance (Brown et al., 2008).

The research study takes into cognizance that earlier studies have found differences between voluntary and mandatory technology acceptance, yet there is a lack of research studies done in which technology acceptance has been thoroughly observed in the mandatory-use context. For the purpose of the study, we excluded the moderating *voluntariness of use* factor as originally suggested by Venkatesh et al. (2003) to focus primarily on mandatory technology acceptance in organizations. Therefore, given the instances in which management consultants might use the WAT in a mandatory work environment, the UTAUT is used in this study in that context to ascertain the acceptance of web analytics by management consultants.

Technology Acceptance Models

When rapid technological advancement changed the landscape of the business environment in the late 1980s, IS researchers continued to develop and improve upon the various models of technology acceptance models to explain the dynamic phenomenon of acceptance. Some of the models are based on the basic assumption that the individual or organization's behavioral intention to accept a technology is a predictor of usage behavior (Hartwick, and Warshaw, 1988; Sheppard, Taylor and Todd, 1995; Ajzen, 1991).

The research studies of Davis et al. (1989) brought the technology acceptance model (TAM) to the limelight, paving the way for diverse scientific research on technology acceptance and usage. This study focuses on the eight reviewed models of the original UTAUT studies to explain the phenomenon of technology acceptance as follows.

Theory of Reasoned Action (TRA)

As far back as 1862, researchers have studied various psychological theories to examine the relationship between attitude and behavior. The TRA model with the two important constructs of attitude toward behavior and the subjective norm was the most effective model used to study human behavior. Fishbein and Ajzen (1975) developed the TRA model from subsequent theories to investigate a means to predict behaviors and outcomes. The TRA mode was constructed based on the assumption that individuals tend to utilize existing information to make judicious decisions, a similar situation that individual users face when it comes to using IS.

With the efforts of IS researchers to explain individual technology acceptance with the TRA model, the critical evaluation of behavioral intentions tends to predict individual performance of any intentional behavior (Ajzen and Madden, 1986). To explain further, the higher the individual intentions, the more certain that an individual will perform an intended behavior. The TRA model takes its premise from the conception of individual intentions, beliefs, and behaviors (Venkatesh et al., 2003; Fishbein and Ajzen, 1975; Ajzen and Fishbein, 1980). Fishbein and Ajzen (1975) further explained that a given attitude (A) toward a behavior tends to be a function of the individual's perception of the behavior's outcome, or the probability that the individual behavior can lead to specific outcomes, along with subjective norms (Ajzen and Fishbein, 1980). According to TRA, the main determinant of a behavior is a behavioral intention, which, sequentially, is determined by *attitude* and *subjective norm,* as illustrated in Figure 2.

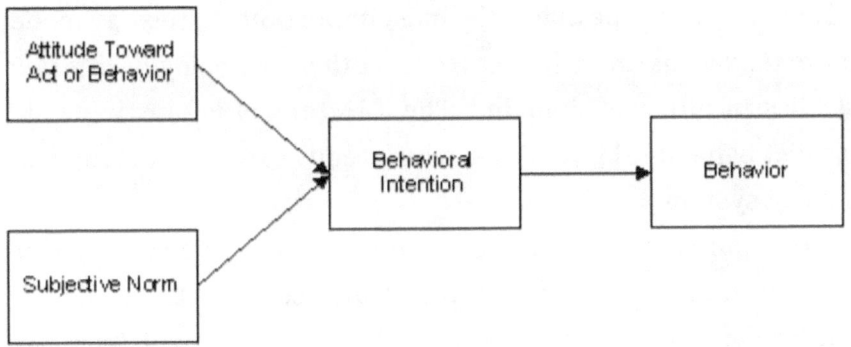

Figure 2. Theory of Reasoned Action (TRA). Adapted from Ajzen and Fishbein, 1980

TRA is one of the most effective theories to explain the concept of consumer behavioral research. The TRA model has been used extensively by business analysts and marketer analysts to study trends and demographic consumer behavior (Sheppard, Hartwick, and Warshaw, 1988). With the study of e-business models, TRA and TAM are important for determining website usage behavior (Davis, 1989; Davis, Bagozzi, and Warshaw, 1989; Fishbein and Ajzen, 1975). Although TRA can help predict individual technology, most researchers agree that combining it with other models makes it more effective, especially in this research study, in which a new technology such as WAT acceptance is being evaluated, which requires an integrated model like UTAUT.

Technology Acceptance Model (TAM, TAM-2 and C-TAM-TPB)

Research studies by Davis (1989) and Davis et al. (1989) led to the development of TAM, a versatile IS research model for predicting IT acceptance and usage with two important constructs: perceived usefulness and perceived ease of use. Over decades, TAM has been found to be one of the most important technology models for extensive use in IS literature and other technology acceptance studies in different domains. The TAM model is mostly used to predict behavioral intentions, which tends to lead to actual use of a given system.

Compared to TRA in IS technology acceptance literature, TAM essentially excluded the attitude constructs of the TRA and replaced it with the "perceived ease of use" and "perceived usefulness" as the major determining factors to evaluate individual behavioral intentions that lead to actual use of systems. Venkatesh and Davis (2000) extended the concept of TAM by introducing a new construct subjective norm in the mandatory environment to create the TAM 2. Most researchers have observed that the TAM predicts *behavioral intentions*, which lead to actual systems usage, and can be considered as a function of *perceived usefulness* and *perceived ease of use*, as indicated in Figure 3.

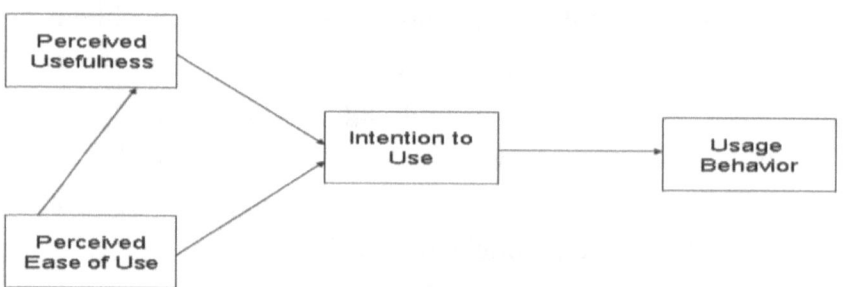

Figure 3. Technology acceptance model (TAM). Adapted from Venkatesh and Davis (2000)

TAM supports the assumption that with the best knowledge of the important determinant of intention to use a given IS system, researchers and IT management can predict system actual usage. In other research studies, it was found that the TRA and TAM can predict system usage with their intention models (Venkatesh et al. 2008; Sheppard, Hartwick, and Warshaw, 1988; Albarracín, Johnson, Fishbein, and Muellerleile, 2001; Venkatesh et al., 2003). Venkatesh et al. (2008) agreed that the robust and reliable scales of TAM exhibits, which have been validated in most IS research studies, can predict relationships that help to evaluate the important determinants of IS intentional usage in different settings (Mathieson, 1991; Adams, Nelson, and Todd, 1992).

Given that advanced technology has evolved rapidly over the years, IS researchers began to question behavioral models like TRA and TAM's inability to predict actual behavior of system usage; rather, it only could predict behavioral intentions (Straub, Keil, and Brenner, 1997). In the research study of Lee et al. (2003), 101 TAM studies were investigated, and significant limitations were found. The use of a convenience sample and a single IS system do not fully reflect the realities of technology usage in an organizational environment. Most IS researchers ascertain that it is difficult for the TAM model to determine the actual usage of a given IS system. This situation prompted new, different models and various extensions like TAM I, TAM II, and TAM III, all of which added to the original TAM. To handle the limitations of TAM, the UTAUT model that takes into account the constructs of other models were selected to make it more robust.

Motivational Model (MM)

Bagozzi, and Warshaw (1992) introduced the motivation theory based on the main constructs of *extrinsic motivation* and *intrinsic motivation* to further explain the concept of technology acceptance and usage. Research studies done on motivational theory revealed the concept that people react differently depending on the contextual setting (Davis et al., 1992; Calder and Staw, 1975; Venkatesh and Speier, 1999). The motivational model emphasizes the essence of social influence that a group can exert on individual behavior.

Vallerand (1997) examined the social influence on individuals with regard to both verbal and nonverbal activities that have a substantial impact on individual decisions with regards to technology acceptance and usage. The greater part of research studies support the claim that the two types of motivation influence human behavior intrinsically and extrinsically. The intrinsic motivation involves the pleasure and satisfaction that can be related to the act of performing by itself, and in this sense, the value of the activity alone is primarily the reward derived by performing. On the flipside, extrinsic motivation provides rewards rather than satisfaction derived just from doing the activity.

Motivational theory advances that both *intrinsic* and *extrinsic motivation* have a significant influence on individual intention to accomplish an activity and the actual performance as well. Davis et al. (1992), in the context of new technology acceptance research studies, found that both intrinsic and extrinsic motivation are key drivers for individual intention to use a technology.

Theory of Planned Behavior (TPB)

Most researchers consider the Theory of Planned Behavior (TPB) as an extension of TRA (Ajzen and Fishbein, 1980). Sheppard et al. (1988), together with most researchers, described the TPB as one of the most dominant theories to explain and predict the phenomenon of behavior expectations in IS literature, and it has been shown to be capable of predicting different variety of behaviors. Most researchers have used TPB as a foundation to explain individual process acceptance and usage in different contexts, which includes technology acceptance (Ajzen, 1991; Ajzen and Schifter, 1985; Mathieson, 1991).

The TPB model with an additional construct of perceived behavioral control was extended by Ajzen (1991). The TRA model provides a profound understanding of the phenomenon of individual technology acceptance and usage (Taylor and Todd, 1995; Mathieson, 1991). Venkatesh et al. (2003) observed that regarding the TPB model, like TAM, the conception of attitude tends to be the subjective norm and perceived behavioral control is considered its underlying belief structure, as shown in Figure 4.

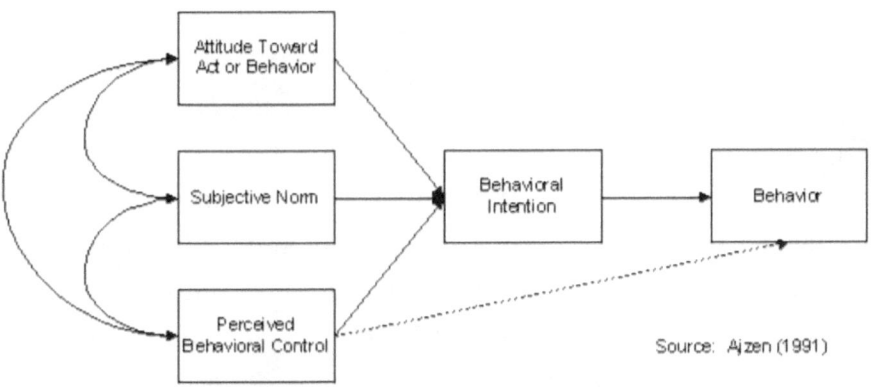

Figure 4. Theory of planned behavior (TPB). Adapted from Ajzen and Schifter (1985); Ajzen (1991)

In particular, Venkatesh et al. (2007) were explicit in explaining that TPB, like other models, encompasses additional constructs including belief factors, factors from related models, and the examination of moderators, as well as the antecedents of the *perceived ease of use* and *perceived usefulness* of the constructs. In effect, the TAM theory is expanded to provide stronger insights to explore the phenomenon of technology acceptance (Wixom and

Todd, 2005). The study of human behavior reveals that most human behaviors can be subjected to hindrances; in this vein, Ajzen (1991) presented the TPB model with an additional construct of perceived behavioral control, which helps to generalize the TRA model. It is important to consider that behavioral intentions are motivational factors that ascertain a quest for individuals to perform a behavior (Ajzen, 1991). The TPB model reveals that the behavioral intention is the most prominent predictor of behavior (Hsiu-Fen, 2010; Albarracín et al., 2001; Sheppard et al., 1988).

Decompose Theory of Planned Behavior (C-TAM-TPB TPB)

The unique characteristic of the C-TAM-TPB TPB is that it incorporates the *predictors of TPB* with *perceived usefulness from TAM*. Certain researchers have studied the impact of different models to understand individual behavioral intention and usage. Under normal circumstances, the TAM and TPB models are combined in order to evaluate the variables of both models and to ascertain the most influential factors (Taylor and Todd, 1995; Mathieson, 1991). In the research studies done by Taylor and Todd (1995), with the moderating variable as experience and the constructs from TAM added in as *perceived usefulness* and *ease of use* to TPB, the model was successful in predicting the behavior of inexperienced users of new technology.

Model of PC Utilization (MPCU)

The model of PC utilization takes its premise from the theory of human behavior according to Triandis (1977), who proposed that behavior is a determinant of attitudes, social norms, habits, and expected consequences of behavior. Triandis further suggested that social factors, effect, and perceived consequences can determine intention and also that intention, facilitating conditions, and habit hierarchies sequentially determine behavior. Triandis (1997) argued that habit hierarchies influence behavior both directly and indirectly by impacting on effect. The important six constructs proposed by Thompson,Higgins, and Howell (1991) include complexity, constructs as *job fit, long-term consequences, affect toward use, social factors, and facilitating conditions* that primarily focus on the IS environment. The model has been used successfully to envisage PC utilization based on the subset of variables of the model proposed by Triandis.

Innovation Diffusion Theory (IDT)

The IDT model ascertains the patterns pertaining to the acceptance process that provides important insights on predicting new technology acceptance. In particular, the SCT model explores five major constructs as *outcome expectations–performance, outcome expectations—personal,* and *self-efficacy* (Compeau and Higgins, 1995). For decades, the concept of Innovation Diffusion Theory, originated by Rogers (1983), has been the foundation of several research studies on diverse forms of innovations. Rogers (1995) underscored that technological innovation exhibits various stages of knowledge, persuasion, decision, implementation, confirmation, and other essential properties.

Most IS researchers recognize the importance of the properties of innovation proposed by the IDT, and as such, Moore and Benbasat (1991) built on this premise with established constructs including *relative advantage, ease of use, image, visibility, compatibility, results demonstrability,* and *voluntariness of use* to examine individual technology acceptance. Several researchers in different studies have attained enough empirical evidence to support the predictive validity of these innovation characteristics and the relationship of the variables proposed by the Moore and Benbasat (1991) model (Plouffe, Hullan, and Vandenbosch, 2001; Agarwal and Prasad, 1997; Karahanna, Straub, and Chervany, 1999). Venkatesh et al. (2003) chose the set of variables based on the Moore and Benbasat (1991) model to develop the UTAUT instead of the original attributes by Rogers (1983) for the intent of the model to be applied to information technologies.

Social Cognitive Theory (SCT)

The SCT model, according to Venkatesh et al. (2003), is one of the most dominant and influential human behavior theories. The SCT is composed of the *core constructs as expectations performance, outcome expectations personal, self-efficacy, affect,* and *social influence* (Bandura, 1986). Social cognitive theory is one of the most acknowledged theories of human behavior (Bandura, 1977). This theory hypothesizes that human behavior can be explained in terms of *triadic reciprocality* whereby behavior, cognition, and other personal factors and environmental events interrelate and end up being the determinants of each other factors.

The important concept of the *triadic reciprocality* is social cognitive theory (SCT), adapted from Compeau and Higgins (1995). SCT takes into account the idea that humans have the capability to control their behaviors, as well as their thinking, beliefs, and feelings, all of which then influence their behavior expectations. This phenomenon includes both concepts of efficacy *expectations and outcome expectations.* In the context of computer utilization, Compeau and Higgins (1995) used the concepts in SCT to explain the linkages among *cognitive factors* (self-efficacy, performance-related outcome expectations, and personal outcome expectations), *affective factors* (affect and anxiety), and *usage.*

Compeau and Higgins (1995) revealed that the construct of self-efficacy tends to judge individual ability to use a technology to accomplish a given task. In the same sense, people are more likely to perform a task that they believe they have the adequate capabilities than the tasks beyond their capabilities. Compeau, Higgins, and Huff (1999) established empirical evidence to establish the relationships among variables. Venkatesh et al. (2003) adapted the Compeau et al. (1999) model instead of the original SCT for the UTAUT because this model is intended to be applied in the context of computer technologies rather than general sociological and psychological applications.

Most IS research studies have built a general consensus that with the limitations of individual technology acceptance models, the initiative to combine more models is ideal for examining the technology acceptance process. The authors of UTAUT cross-examined all the prevailing technology acceptance models with a longitudinal research study involving six organizations over a six-month period. In the light of these studies, the UTAUT model proposed by Venkatesh et al. (2003) combines the elements across the eight models. The following presents a detailed review of the core constructs in each of the eight models.

UTAUT Model

In 2003, Venkatesh, Morris, Davis, and Davis established UTAUT, which identified eight main competing theoretical models. Then they validated the new model in a longitudinal study with results that account for 70 percent of the variance in usage intention

(Venkatesh et al., 2003). It is important to recognize that the UTAUT model has contributed to important IS research findings that have shaped understanding of technology acceptance process. The initial purpose of UTAUT was to help the authors provide an explanation of one's behavioral intentions to use a given IS and to predict successive usage behavior, yet IS researchers have used the UTUAT model in diverse studies. IS literature presents various kinds of IS models for technology acceptance, and this study uses the UTAUT model by Venkatesh et al. (2003) as the fundamental theoretical framework to analyze web analytic technology acceptance in the context of management consulting. Additionally, most IS research studies done using the UTAUT model found the main constructs as robust for the study of new technology acceptance (Wang, Wang, and Wu, 2009).

The authors of the UTAUT model began an intensive investigation of all the compelling technology acceptance models to find important trends and shortfalls of the previous models. The outcome of this strict scrutiny of IS literature on technology acceptance is the proposed four fundamental constructs, namely: performance expectancy, effort expectancy, social influence, and facilitating conditions. And they have significant determination of usage intention and behavior (Venkatesh et al., 2003). The studies equally confirmed that the concept of understanding usage as a dependent variable is essential for predicting IS usage behavioral expectations. Furthermore, out of all seven moderating factors used in the original research studies by Venkatesh et al. (2003), gender, age, experience, and voluntariness seem to have a significant impact on the four key constructs involving usage intention and behavior. The remaining three moderation factors of attitude, self-efficacy, and anxiety did not have a significant influence on intention to use a given IS, as indicated in Figure 5.

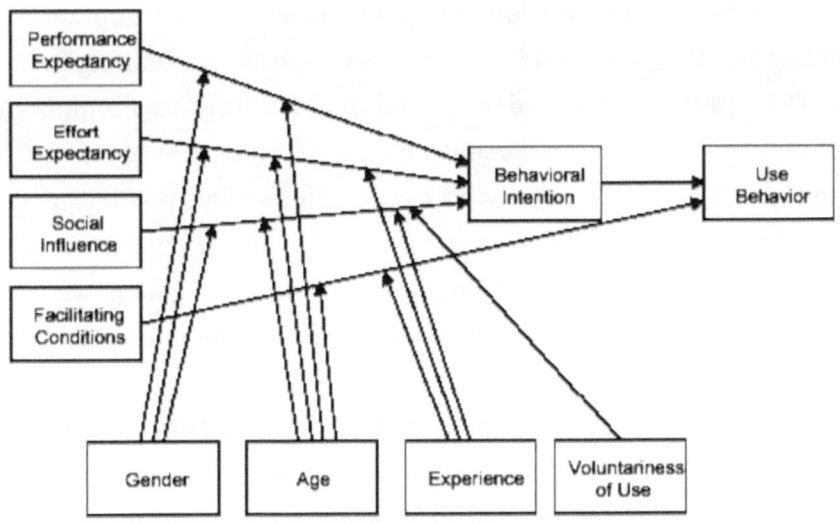

Figure 5. Unified theory of technology acceptance and use (UTAUT). Adapted from Venkatesh et al. (2003).

IS researchers over the last four decades have developed and tested several theoretical models in an endeavor to explain the phenomenon of technology acceptance and usage. The rising need to understand technology acceptance, by both practitioners and researchers, necessitates coming up with a model that can keep up with the fast pace of technology advancement. More importantly, in order for organizations to attain success with technology implementation, there is the need for employees to accept and be willing to use IT to improve efficiency. One of the most well-researched areas in IS literature is the evaluation of the return on investment in IT implementation accounting for user acceptance of IT.

The Main Constructs of UTAUT

For the past four decades, IS researchers have successfully developed multiple models to explain IT user behavior to enhance an effective implementation of IT policies in various organizations (Zweig and Webster, 2003). UTAUT, as proposed by Venkateshet et al., 2003 presents a broader spectrum that integrates important constructs of previous research on technology acceptance to examine IT user behavior and expectations. The UTAUT model incorporates several models for building a stronger base to analyze the determinants of technology acceptance and usage and for providing profound explanations for the technology acceptance process in different contexts.

Most of IS research studies confirmed the notion that the use of several models have greater propensity to provide adequate explanations and predictions of user acceptance of IT; UTAUT is the most predictive (Venkatesh et al., 2003; Davis, Baggozzi, and Warshaw 1989). Since the initial research studies in 2003 that underscored the reliability of UTAUT as a research model, several researchers have tested the important constructs of the UTAUT in varied research environments (Brown, Dennis, and Venkatesh, 2010). The robustness of the UTAUT model enables researchers to test it in a diverse environment, with new technology and in certain circumstances to add important constructs to it. The main goal of this research study is to test UTAUT in the context of the management consulting industry and with new technology web analytics.

Therefore, it was logical to expect that the use of the UTAUT as a theoretical base would be more beneficial to investigate the important determinants of web analytic technology acceptance in the context of management consulting. The authors of UTAUT advocated for the further development and validation of the model in different environments and most especially with the study of new technologies. In this vein, the research study adopts UTAUT as the theoretical framework, for the model presents a comprehensive and broader spectrum to examine web analytic technology acceptance in the context of management consulting. Thus, the research study further hypothesizes that the relationships between the determinants and behavioral intention would be moderated by age, gender, and experience. The fourth moderating factor, as voluntary, was excluded, because the study focuses mainly on the context of mandatory environment.

Based on the Vankatesh et al. (2003) studies, in this research undertaking, four constructs were adapted: performance expectancy, effort expectancy, social influence, and facilitating conditions as the important determinants of behavioral intention (BI) to use web analytic technology. It is essential to note that in previous IS research studies done on these four core technology acceptance beliefs, the generalizability of these constructs to the acceptance of various technologies in both voluntary and mandatory settings could be established (Zhang, 2010; Venkatesh et al., 2003; Chen et al., 2007; Venkatesh). These four important constructs have been tested and validated in diverse research studies in different context of technology applications.

Performance Expectation

Venkateshet al. (2003) explained that construct performance expectancy is the extent to which individual users believe that utilizing a given IS will enable them to realize benefits in job performance. Regarding previous IS research studies, the performance expectation takes its premises from five main constructs of eight different models, known as jobfit (MPCU), (TAM/TAM2 and C-TAM-TAB), extrinsic motivation (MM), relative advantage (IDT), and outcome expectations (SCT). Venkatesh et al. and previous researchers considered that performance expectancy is the strongest predictor of IT intentional behavior and subsequent usage (Taylor and Todd, 1995; Compeau and Higgins, 1995; Davis et al., 1989). Several IS research studies provide substantial evidence to support the claim that performance expectancy can predict user intention to use any given information system (Deng, Liu, and Qi, 2011; Abushanab and Pearson, 2007; Van Raaij and Schepers, 2008; Eckhardt, Laumer, and Weitzel, 2009).

Venkatesh et al. (2009) defined performance expectancy as the extent to which a management consultant believes that using web analytics technology (WAT) will help him or her to attain gains in the performance, creating value for their clients and knowing that important determinants of web analytics technology will be beneficial. WAT will be beneficial because management consultants can synchronize and integrate real-time information to existing data to enable fast and agile strategic decision-making processes to advise clients on critical business issues. In another sense, performance expectancy is the extent to which an individual user perceives that using a system will enable him or her to increase productivity and efficiency, which is conceptually and empirically similar to the construct of perceived usefulness. Therefore, the proposed hypothesis based on performance expectation follows.

Effort Expectancy

Similar to performance expectation, the definition provided by Venkatesh et al. (2003) for effort expectancy is the extent of ease associated with the use of a given system. To explain it further in the context of the research study, it is the extent of ease regarding the use of web analytic technology. Researchers have confirmed the similarities of the three constructs from the different models as perceived ease of use (TAM/TAM2), complexity (MPCU), and ease of use (IDT), which form the basic foundation of effort expectancy (Thompson, Higgins, and Howell, 1991; Davis et al., 1989; Plouffe et al., 2001). The studies of Vankatesh et al. (2003) suggested that effort expectancy tends to be a weak predictor in UTAUT with an $R2$ ranging from .08-.2, $p<.05$. The concept of effort expectancy is the extent to which using a system is effortless or less demanding. It is empirically similar to the construct of perceived ease proposed by TAM. There seems to be a number of researchers with the perspective that the intention to use an information system is determined by effort expectancy (Van Raaiji and Schepers, 2008; Abushanab and Pearson, 2007; Eckhardt et al., 2009).

Social Influence

Society in general tends to shape individual behavioral expectations and attitudes based on traditional norms and beliefs. Venkatesh et al (2003) asserted that social influences are stronger factors to impact individual intentions to use new technology, with a definition of social influence as the extent to which individuals perceive that important others think that they might use new technology. Although most research studies posit that social influence might not explicitly enact a direct effect on attitude or satisfaction, other researchers believe that the notion of individual satisfaction could be based on conception of internalization and identification (Kelman, 1958).

Prior researchers support the claim that social influence as a variable has a substantial impact on individual intent to use a new technology due to attained satisfaction by conformity and identification (Moore and Benbasat, 1991; Venkatesh and Davis, 2000). There is also substantial evidence that normative beliefs might equally influence attitude (Schepers and Wetzels, 2007;

Ryan, 1982). With regards to user satisfaction, which could be studied as an attitude, it is imperative to expect social influence to have a positive influence on user satisfaction (Brown, Massey, Montoya-Weiss, and Burkman, 2002).

Venkatesh et al.'s (2003) research studies confirmed that the effect of social influence tends to be stronger in mandatory-use environment reasons because individuals in a given work environment have the tendency to comply with IT policies initiated by the senior management team. The latter's authority enables them to exert pressure on effective IT policy implementation in a mandatory setting. Several researchers share the same opinion that the individual intention to use an information system might be determined by social influence (Eckhardt et al., 2009; Abushanab and Pearson, 2007).

Facilitating Conditions

IS research studies provide empirical evidence to support the notion that IS user environment settings is an important element for IS usage success. In this sense, facilitating conditions tend to have a direct impact on intention and use of IS (Taylor and Todd, 1995; Venkatesh et al., 2003). Regarding Festinger's (1957) study on dissonance theory, it is important to note that individual users might adjust their negative attitude to any unfavorable environment. Conversely, given the situation of a favorable environment with adequate resources and support, it is more likely for the individual user to have confidence and positive attitude usage behavior. Another important aspect of facilitating conditions is the notion that mandatory use settings have a significant impact on IT user behavior because the individual user is obliged to use all available resources to be successful (Sykes, Venkatesh, and Gosain, 2009).

Vankatesh et al. (2003) explained facilitating conditions as how individual users perceive that the accessibility of organizational and technical resources to support use of the target system. Vankatesh et al. established that facilitating conditions are great predictors of IT usage behavior in UTAUT with an R2 ranging from .05-.18, p<.05. The researcher considers facilitating conditions as the extent to which individual users believe that the existing organizational and technical infrastructure to support the use of web analytics technology. The proposed hypothesis based on facilitating condition follows.

Moderating Factors

The researchers took into account the influences of three other variables: gender, age, and experience. The fourth variable, voluntariness, was excluded on the direct determinants as moderators. The research of Venkatesh et al. (2003) presented the essence of considering potential moderating factors of user acceptance of technology. In this light, the researcher further proposed that the moderating factors of age, gender, and experience would significantly impact the important determinants and behavioral intentions of WAT acceptance. Based on the four moderating factors in the original UTAUT, this researcher used the moderating factors of age, gender, and experience and excluded voluntariness.

The Moderating Variable—Gender

The important construct of gender as a major demographic variable has attracted the interest of IS researchers in finding the impact of gender differences in the area of IT acceptance.

Research studies done by several authors have provided enough evidence to substantiate the claim that males exhibit more potential positive attitudes toward computing than their female counterparts (Dambrot et al., 1985; Gefen and Straub, 1997; Harrison and Rainer, 1992; Venkatesh, Morris, Sykes, and Ackerman, 2004; Venkatesh, Morris, and Ackerman, 2000). Regarding the known gender differences in IS acceptance, for gender roles, Venkatesh et al. (2003) studied the phenomenon of performance expectancy supporting that men usually exhibit more task-oriented accomplishments than women. To complement the research findings of gender roles and socialization, different societal expectations for men and women provide the explanation of the different assigned roles to men and women (Bem, 1981; Bem and Allen, 1974; Kirchmeyer, 1997; Kirchmeyer, 2002; Lynott and McCandless, 2000; Motowidlo, 1982; Whitely, 1997).

The Moderating Variable—Age

Extensive IS research studies done on the impact of the variable of age on technology acceptances have shown that age differences have a significant influence on technology acceptance (Czaja and Sharit, 1998; Venkatesh et al., 2003; Venkatesh and Morris, 2000; White and Weatherall, 2000). Studies have been done that confirm the impact of differences in age group on IS acceptance with regards to job expectations, attitude, and continuous improvement. It is eminent that young people can more easily accept new technologies than older colleagues can, as claimed by Ellis and Allaire (1999) and earlier researchers (Igbaria and Parashuraman, 1996; Laguna and Babcock, 1997; Wang, 2010). Even though older people exhibit positive attitudes toward computers, at the same time, they tend to have less confidence in them compared to their younger counterparts.

The older people tend to encounter more trouble in general in accepting new technology than younger individuals do. It is then natural to maintain that age as a variable will have a negative correlation with computer knowledge (Dyck and Smither, 1994; Rhodes, 1983).

The Moderating Variable—Experience

The successful implementation of IS projects in organizations depends on continuous training of employees to empower them with the needed skills and competence to realize the full benefit of IS. It is evident that with time, employees will gain the requisite experience to deliver value in the organization with IS (Cornell, Eining, and Hu, 2011; Messineo and DeOllos, 2005). Jiang et al.'s (2003) study confirmed that both important skills and skill proficiency levels are vital in relationship to the system's success, and as a result, employees need to understand the level of skills and importance of the system in order for them to be satisfied with the system. Jay and Willis (1992) explained the relationship experience with computers and attitude change in that attitudes toward computers change due to the nature of experience. Venkatesh et al.'s (2003) study identified the effect of experience on the determinant, which might decline with time.

Limitations of the UTAUT Model

Despite the confirmed robustness of the UTAUT model and its intensive usage in diverse research endeavors, certain researchers, including the authors of the model themselves, identified important limitations to consider. UTAUT as a research model is fairly new, and as recommended by the authors, more research studies are needed to replicate and extend the model further (Berthon, Pitt, Ewing, and Carr, 2002; Venkatesh et al., 2003). Venkatesh et al. (2003) have validated the constructs and the scales used in longitudinal research studies involving multiple organizational settings, yet more research studies can validate them even further.

Furthermore, UTAUT has been validated in successive IS research, but it is obvious that there is still more room for further research studies to account for the 30 percent unexplained acceptance (Baron, Patterson, and Harris, 2006), and to justify the invariance of the UTAUT scales in relation to different cultures, subpopulations, and self- management of learning (Pu-Li and Kishore, 2006; Venkatesh et al., 2003; Venkatesh and Morris, 2000; Venkatesh et al., 2000). Under these conditions, replicating the model with a new WAT in a different research context of management consulting is justified in order to extend our understanding of technology acceptance.

Another important factor to recognize is that the UTAUT model comprises many models and studies on technology acceptance. It is not exhaustive by itself, given the fact that it excludes important individual technology acceptance constructs, such as perceived playfulness and self-motivation, that may be important predictors of IT usage (Cody- Allen and Kishore, 2006). The limitations of the model, not including other important constructs, make it essential for researchers to examine other models to determine if the UTAUT model is the best fit for the research studies. The critical evaluation of all the IS models for technology acceptance is eminent in ascertaining the relevance of each model for a given research work.

In general, numerous research studies confirmed the efficiency and robustness of the UTAUT model to predict individual technology acceptance and use; thus, the motivation for its use for this study.

The comprehensive nature of the model provides a better change to evaluate important determinants of technology acceptance and to investigate the influence of the moderation factors on the main constructs. The original model has a greater tendency to provide further explanation and predictions about individual acceptance of technological innovations in organizations, yet with time, IS researchers have tested and validated UTAUT in different research environments.

Studies Using the UTAUT

The original research instruments of the UTAUT model have been validated in numerous research studies, and the constructs have been replicated with diverse technologies and with different theoretical perspectives. The initial development of the UTAUT model by Venkatesh et al. (2003) was to explain and predict the acceptance of technological innovations in organizations, and afterward, IS researchers have tested and validated UTAUT in different research environments. Various replications and extensions of the UTAUT model have provided essential insights into better understanding technology acceptance. In the most recent IS technology acceptance literature, researchers have either used all or certain important constructs of the UTUAT model to test and validate emerging technologies against traditionally accepted technologies from both individual and group user perspectives.

Cultural Background

Given the fact that the concept of globalization and technology exert great influence on business operations, the culture phenomenon plays an important role in studies of technology acceptance. There is sufficient empirical evidence that different cultural expectations can limit or enhance technology usage (Moore and Benbasat, 1991). IS literature provides empirical evidence used to test and validate UTAUT in international settings, and this process has provided a profound understanding of the impact of culture on technology acceptance (Bandyopadhyay and Fraccastoro, 2007).

For the fact that organizations still face the challenges of complex cultural expectations due to globalization, using the UTAUT model with cultural factors presents better insights in understanding the important determinants of technology acceptance and usage across different nations (Im, Hong, and Kang, 2011). Venkatesh and Zhang's (2010) research studies compared UTAUT constructs with similar organizational environments in China and the United States, and the findings highlighted the different perspectives of cultural and societal influence, both individualist and collective, for technology acceptance.

Similarly, Oshlyansky, Cairns, and Thimbleby's (2007) research studies involved nine countries, in an attempt to validate UTAUT across cultures. The results indicated that cultural differences among countries have significant impact on technology acceptance. Currently, the study of Nistor, Göğüş, and Lerche (2013) validates the UTAUT model with a larger research sample (N = 4,589) across three European countries, namely, Germany, Romania, and Turkey, in the context of technology acceptance in an educational setting. The results confirmed the reliability and the validity of the model across culture.

Moreover, the findings of Al-Gahtani, Hubona, and Wang (2007) supported the concept that culture has a significant effect on acceptance using desktop applications in Saudi Arabia. The modified UTAUT accounted for 39.1 percent of intention to use and

42.1 percent of usage variances. Other researchers, such as Cody-Allen and Kishore (2006), extended the UTAUT model to capture cultural variables information. The authors achieved this objective by adding new constructs such as trusting beliefs, information and system quality (ISQ), and information and system satisfaction. Evidently, the significance of the UTAUT model as a theoretical framework provides important insights for understanding the process of WAT, especially in the context of management consulting.

Business Situations

IS researchers over the last four decades have developed and tested several theoretical models to attempt to explain use and acceptance of technology. Venkatesh et al. (2003) originally developed the theoretical framework of the UTAUT model to explain and predict the acceptance of technological innovations in organizations. Yet, in time, IS researchers tested and validated UTAUT in different research environments.

With the original UTAUT model used in the organizational context to explain the determinants of technology acceptance, more research studies were done in different organizational settings. Since its development in 2003, the UTAUT model has been applied by others in a variety of organizational settings (Callaway, 2011; Eckhardt et al., 2009; Koivimäki, Ristola, and Kesti, 2008; Verhoeven, Heerwegh, and De Wit, 2010; Yu Shan, Tsai Fang, Chin Feng, Chien, and Chin Cheh, Y. 2011).

Furthermore, Brown, Dennis, and Venkatesh (2010) developed a new model based on UTAUT that synthesizes research studies on technology adoption and collaboration technology. The study provided a mandate for the design of collaboration technologies that can enhance adoption. Another example of generalizability of UTAUT is the research studies of Venkatesh et al. (2008), which extended the UTAUT model with consumer acceptance and use of information, and an additional construct as communication technology (ICT). Pu-Li and Kishore (2006) validated UTAUT constructs by studying web log systems, and Taiwo and Downe (2013) used a meta- analysis method to investigate the existing empirical literatures on UTAUT with a larger population sample (*N* =11000). The results indicated that among the five constructs, performance expectation and behavioral intention exhibited a strong relationship, but the others were significant with weak relationships. Carlsson, Carlsson, Hyvonen, Puhakainen, and Waiden (2006) applied the UTAUT model to examine the acceptance of wireless mobile communication in Europe. These research studies explain technology acceptance in the context of organization.

Thus, the UTAUT model presents a theoretical framework for analyzing Internet technologies and how they impact business operations. The research studies on Internet technologies and the UTAUT model (e.g., mobile Internet acceptance, online banking, mobile services acceptance, e-commerce, software applications, social networking, ERP, and management theory) identified significant determinants of technology acceptance (Zhou, Lu, and Wang, 2010; Fillion, Braham,and Ekionea, 2010; Eckhardt et al., 2009; Foon and Fah, 2011; Minishi-Majanja and Dulle, 2011; Sutanonpaiboon and Pearson, 2006; Sykes et al., 2009; Van Raaij and Schepers, 2008; Chong,2012; Wymer and Regan, 2006; Yu Shan et al., 2011; Abushanab and Pearson, 2007; Alwahaishi, and Snášel, 2013). IS researchers have obtained significant empirical evidence to support the UTAUT model in both the context of organizational environment and individual behavior to predict technology acceptance.

The extensive research studies done to validate the constructs of UTAUT in varied contextual research environments make UTAUT more satisfactory to current technology acceptance researchers. San and Ángel (2012) explored the technology acceptance process in the rural tourism industry using UTUAT, and the results of the research study supported the robustness of the UTAUT model constructs. All these research studies make account for either individual behavior or group behavior toward a given technology in a particular research setting. Evidently, the significance of the UTAUT model as a theoretical framework provides important insights for understanding the process of WAT, especially in the context of management consulting.

E-government

In the context of e-government, West (2004) and other researchers presented four distinct facets of the Internet as the online interface of the government for providing services to the general public (Vishanth, Ramzi, Faris, Mahmud, and Yogesh, 2013; Ke and Wei, 2004; Chan et al., 2010; Rivera and Rogers, 2004; Layne and Lee, 2001). The initial stage is the *billboard stage*, which serves as an interface for government to provide essential information to the public. The web acceptance literature mentions firms that have minimum web presence, as their websites just offer basic company information about the organization. The next stage enables public access to information from government websites with limited online services, and the third stage, in addition, provides fully integrated online services to the public.

The unique characteristic of the final stage of the e-government interface according to West (2004) is that government websites make use of extensive advanced Internet technologies in the form of interactive websites with self-services for the public. The fully integrated websites not only provide instant services to the public but also use other Internet technologies to enrich the websites' content with user feedback. Chan et al. (2010) explained that all of the stages are important in the planning and implementation of IT strategies to make the e-government effective and efficient.

Because all the stages have differences conceptualizations regarding the deployment process, the overall consensus in the IS literature supports the claim that strategic planning must take into cognizance all the important aspects of the different stages.

Researchers have explored the UTAUT model to investigate the important determinants of e-government acceptance. The research work done in the area of study of e-government has established that the UTUAT model provides significant empirical evidence to explain much of the variance. Loo, Yeow, and Chong (2009) used the UTAUT model to explain to what extent the user accepts the national identity card (NIC) and driving license (DL) applications, which are both integrated into the Malaysian government multipurpose smartcard. The findings indicated that constructs like lack of understanding of benefits, anxiety about damaging the hardware, and lack of social support and credibility explained the low intention of people to use the new technology. A Wang and Shih (2009) research study on acceptance of informational kiosks as a technology validated the UTAUT model, and in the same instances, Al-Awadhi and Morrison's (2008) studies on the e-government in Kuwait signified that the behavioral intention to use the e-government is determined by factors including performance expectancy, peer influence, effort expectancy, and facilitating conditions.

The UTAUT model in the context of e-government has provided significant insight into understanding technology acceptance in government administration. In the context of e-government, Chan et al. (2010) used UTAUT as a theoretical framework to examine the important determinants of smartcard use to identify citizens who have access to e-government services. The research studies emphasized technology acceptance a mandatory environment. The authors explored the modalities of the four- stage model of new technology to identify eight external factors, including: *awareness, assistance, convenience, self-efficacy, trust, avoidance of personal interaction, flexibility*, and *compatibility*. The findings of the study supported previous research studies in which three core constructs of UTAUT: performance expectancy, facilitating conditions, and effort expectancy, have a significant influence on citizens' satisfaction with smartcards.

The present study builds on the constructs of previous studies done on Internet acceptance, with a focus on how the organizations could unleash all the potential benefits of websites to create value. It explores the fourth stage of the website deployment process presented by West (2004) to identify the important determinants of WAT acceptance in the context of management consulting. Most essentially, the UTAUT model, which encompasses several IS technology models, enabled this study to broaden understanding of the significant drivers of WAT acceptance and the effect of moderating factors in the context of the management consulting industry.

IS literature on Internet acceptance places much emphasis on how Internet technologies have transformed global business operations to reflect the realities of global markets. WAT is essential in the sense that organizations have access to web data from the activities of customers as well as business partners to create sustainable relationship management. This process enhances effective collaboration and exchange of vital information to meet business expectations. Because no significant research studies exist on WAT acceptance in the context of management consulting industry, the research study explored the determinants of WAT acceptance with the UTUAT model presented by Venkatesh et al. (2003).

Educational Settings

Another important area of research for which the UTAUT model has been used extensively is education. Important IS research studies conducted on how technology impacts education delivery from the point of view of learners, instructors, and administrators have extended our understanding of technology acceptance (Lin and Anol, 2008; Birch and Irvine, 2009; Van Schaik, 2009; Hsiao-Hui, 2012; Marchewka and Liu, 2007; Moran, 2006; Tao, 2011; Koivimäki et al., 2008; Lewis, Fretwell, Ryan, and Parham, 2013). Moran (2006) applied the UTAUT model to assess college students' acceptance of tablet PCs. The study supported the ability of the model to determine individual intention to use a given technology.

Similarly, Anderson et al. (2006) used the UTAUT model to evaluate drivers for tablet PCs acceptance by faculty in a college of business. The concept of e-learning and new technologies for enhancing the educational process for both students and professors have also been used to explain the individual behavioral technology acceptance process. All these research studies account for either individual behavior or group behavior toward a given technology in a particular research setting. It is fair to say that more research studies might be done over a certain period of time to establish the strong generalizability of the model.

Professional Environment

The phenomenon of advanced technology dominating the twenty-first century global business environment has mandated that individual professionals acquire innovative IT applications to enhance their core competencies to create value for the customer. Amid fierce global competition, organizations explore an effective technology management to empower individual professionals to meet industry expectations. IS literature on technology acceptance in the context of professionals presents different perceptions and variations depending on industry expectations. The conclusions made by Goodhue and Thompson (1995) placed more emphasis on the importance of the task context and the element of non-routineness. Additional factors, such as peer influence, significantly influence individual technology acceptance in a professional setting.

Research studies on technology acceptance in a professional context offer different industry-specific findings to extend our understanding of this acceptance. Dowling (2008) admitted that different types of technology are deployed in the audit profession that demands special consideration. This challenge requires different IS models to examine the multiple facet of technology and the different audit firms with various aspects of business operations (Curtis and Payne, 2008; Loraas and Wolf, 2006). Rowe (2008) and other studies on professionals have found that technology acceptance is more significant in evaluating team effectiveness.

The research studies on information technology as it enhances professional job expectations have made it more relevant in a technology-driven economy. It is important to observe that researchers in the health sciences have used the UTAUT model to extend understanding of technology acceptance in the medical profession (Lee and Rho, 2013; Chang, Hwang, Hung, and Li, 2006; Hennington and Janz, 2007). Chau and Hu's (2002) studies empirically examined telemedicine technology acceptance by physicians using data of more than 400 physicians at public tertiary hospitals in Hong Kong. Subsequently, in the results of the research studies, new insights to understand technology acceptance by individual professionals are provided. Wills, El-Gayar, and Bennett (2008) explored the UTAUT model to explain healthcare professionals' acceptance of electronic medical records; the findings proved the capability of UTAUT as a research model for assessing technology acceptance among professionals. As indicated, the social influence construct tends to be a significant determinant of intention to use technology in settings of the medical profession.

Following the trend of technology acceptance of professionals that involve the examination of a specific technology, a specific professional (user) category, or both, this researcher investigated the important determinants and the significant moderating factors of WAT acceptance in the context of professional management consultants. In a broader sense, given the fact that technology acceptance studies vary with regards to technology and professional categories, this study might expand understanding of technology acceptance of professional management consultants with new streams of research for future studies.

Conclusion

The present literature review of individual technology acceptance builds knowledge based on understanding how individuals perceive technology given the case that individual management consultants tend to exhibit such characteristics. Because employees often play a major role in the successful implementation of new technologies in organizations, it is important to understand the most important determinants and how the moderating factors impact technology acceptance and usage for effective managerial decisions. Studies of Internet technology acceptance equally indicate all the important factors that influence individual perceptions about technology. Internet technologies present greater opportunities for business to attain organic growth by meeting the expectations of the global market. The review of the UTAUT model and how it is being successfully used in various IS studies make it an essential tool for the study in filling the IS literature gap, most especially in the area of the management consulting industry to determine WAT. The next chapter presents the scientific methodology and the statistical analysis used to undertake this research study.

CHAPTER 3

Methodology

Introduction

This chapter outlines the research methodology and theoretical perspectives of the research study. It presents the research design and the theoretical framework that the research study builds upon. The section explains the characteristics of population under study, the sample size, and the instruments used to collect the data. The sections also include the description of the procedure for data collection and statistical instruments used to analyze the data. Finally, the chapter describes necessary measures taken to validate the reliability of the selected instrument and the ethical considerations to govern the entire research study process.

Research Design

The general overview of the research study maintains a positivist stance with a quantitative methodology and the use of an objective approach to examine the relationship between the given constructs. The research design consists of a quantitative research study with the use of an online survey research technique. The research design includes a cross-sectional survey study that gathers online survey data at a single point in time. The study is exploratory in nature in the sense that little is known about the drivers of WAT acceptance among management consultants.

The researcher used SurveyMonkey as a tool to administer the survey to the population sample randomly selected from the United States. The survey instrument was sent to prospective participants through e-mail that included a secure embedded hyperlink and a password to access the survey. The survey research technique can determine the attributes of large populations with a given sample of the entire population (Babbie, 2000; Fowler, 2009).

Because one of the goals of the study is to test the UTAUT model in a different research context, the researcher adapted the survey instrument used in the research studies of Venkatesh et al. (2003). The survey instrument was used as a research tool to gather data from management consultants who use technology for their daily work expectations. The main objective of gathering the data was to enable the researcher to make inferences about the population's behavioral intentions to use WAT and to attain enough empirical evidence to reject or accept the proposed hypotheses. The online survey research technique, with advanced research technology provided by SurveyMonkey, can help to determine the attributes of large populations with a given sample of the entire population (Babbie, 2000). The researcher used statistical tools including regression analysis and the Statistical Package for Statistical for Social Science (SPSS 18.0) to analyze the data.

The research study explored quantitative methodology and online survey techniques to determine WAT acceptance. Creswell (2009) noted that quantitative methodology offers numerous advantages as opposed to qualitative methodology, especially in the area of measuring relationships among factors. Using a quantitative method is important to determine the relationship between the variables that impact the user acceptance of technology innovations. Additionally, the online survey techniques presented more advantages than traditional paper-and-pencil surveys do in the sense that the data collection is more timely, available all day and every day, accurate, easy to be uploaded into analysis software packages; it is also globally reaching, easy to follow up, and low in cost (Babbie, 2000; Cooper and Schindler, 2008; Marrelli, 2004).

The online survey technique approach enabled the researcher to use SurveyMonkey, a vendor's administrative tool, to collect data from the participants. All the participants received an e-mail that provided the consent information and an embedded hyperlink to access the password-protected survey instruments. The participants then had access to the survey instruments, and after completion, the data were sent to a secured database. The researcher reloaded the data to a statistical tool, SPSS, for data analysis within a secured computing environment to protect the information of the participants. According to Fowler (2009), the online survey technique offers enough flexibility for the participants to take the survey at their own convenient time because it is available all day and every day, easy, and user friendly. There was a second round of e-mails sent to the participants as a friendly reminder to complete the survey and to increase participation.

Population and Sample

The population choice for the purpose of the study is US management consultants. The management industry consists of both large and small firms that operate in the local, national, and global market. Management consultant firms provide services to organizations to help the management leaders in areas of marketing, operations, leadership, human resources, project management, and technology innovations. The researcher contacted a representative at SurveyMonkey, a company with more than three million panelists who are willing to take part in various kinds of surveys. To meet the specific research requirements, SurveyMonkey has the capability to profile its members with more than five hundred attributes. The representative was able to find 1,500 management consultant prospects in their database, and a minimum of 218 consultants were targeted for the research project.

The researcher used a commercial online survey service known as SurveyMonkey to recruit and to administer the online survey tool prospective participants. SurveyMonkey has more than 3 million members who participate in a variety of research studies. Its members represent the national population, and they are profiled according to 500 attributes (SurveyMonkey, 2013). The researcher established initial contacts to get the necessary authorizations and permission to collect data from a SurveyMonkey survey panel. The data collection methods adhered strictly to the procedures outlined in the Capella University Institutional Review Board (IRB). SurveyMonkey sent e-mails to the individuals who met the initial screening criteria. The participants used up to ten minutes to finish the survey questionnaires, and after a week, the participants received another e-mail as a reminder and a note of appreciation for completing the study. The link was closed afterward that no one could access the study afterward. The data was secured, including the backup data, and protected with a password.

The research study uses the formula proposed by Brightman and Schneider (1994) to ascertain the statistical probabilistic sample size. The formula is explained as follows:

$n = (z2\ p\ (1-p))/E2$

Where,

n = Sample size for the study,

z = Value of the specified confidence interval,

p = Percentage of the survey questionnaires that were turned in, and

E = Maximum tolerable error or degree of precision.

This researcher used the degree of confidence level of 95 percent or a *z* value of 1.96, which indicates a chosen for the degree of confidence value of +/- 5 percent as the degree of precision. The selected *p* value is 0.10, which is based on the reported 10 percent mail survey return up to a maximum of 19 percent (Dillman, 2000; Pelosi et al., 2001).

The value of *n* is :

$$n = (1.96^2(.10)\ (1-.10))/.05^2 = 138$$

Because the representative of SurveyMonkey was able to identify 1,500 management consultant survey membership panelists that met the search requirement, a 20 percent return rate might have yielded about three hundred completed questionnaires that would be within the calculated sample size. The minimum target population was 218 management consultants. The researcher used a sample-size calculator (http://www.raosoft.com/samplesize.html) to ascertain the required minimum sample size.

Setting

The main objective of the research study was to identify the significant determinants of WAT by management consultants, establish existing relationships, and find out how the moderating factors including age, gender, and experience impact the main determinants. The researcher intended to use management consultants in both large and small organization consultants firms that provide services to organizations to help management teams in areas of marketing, operation, leadership, human resources, project management, and technology innovations. To meet the requirement of the research study, the researcher engaged the services of SurveyMonkey to recruit and to administer the online survey tool to the participants who were willing to take part in the study (SurveyMonkey, 2013).

SurveyMonkey, considered as a leading research company, has more than 3 million members who participate in a variety of research studies. SurveyMonkey's members represent the national population and there are five hundred attributes to profile the participants. Using attributes including management consultants operating in the United States to identify potential participants, the representative of SurveyMonkey identified about 1,500 management consultants who were likely to partake in the study and the minimum target population of 218 management consultants. The project manager from the SurveyMonkey ensured that an invitation e-mail was sent to all potential participants who met the initial screening criteria to request their participation in the study (SurveyMonkey, 2013).

Instrumentation / Measures

The researcher adopted the original instrument used by Venkatesh et al. (2003), and then the only changes made were to replace the word *system* with *WAT*. Regarding the instrument of Venkatesh et al. (2003), since its inception, certain researchers have used it in numerous studies, and it has been proved to be valid and reliable (Alawadhi and Morris, 2008; Bandyopadhyay and Fraccastoro, 2007; Carlsson et al., 2006; Venkatesh et al., 2003). One of the advantages of using a preexisting instrument is that the items have already been designed and tested for validation. The variables were ordinal with a seven-point Likert scale described as follows: 1. Strongly disagree, 2. Moderately disagree, 3. Slightly disagree, 4. Neutral, 5. Slightly agree, 6. Moderately agree, and 7. Strongly agree.

Data Collection

The target population for this study was management consultants in both small and large corporations in the United States. The participants who were eligible for the studies had to be at least eighteen years of age or older, and there were no restrictions on gender or ethnicity. The data from the target population were appropriate for the objective of this study. However, to effectively reach the target population, the researcher contracted the online commercial survey company SurveyMonkey, which has more than 3 million membership panelists willing to take various kinds of surveys (SurveyMonkey, 2013). In addition to the fact that most of the members are spread across the nation, SurveyMonkey has the capability of profiling its members with more than 500 attributes, which allows researchers to target particular individuals based on research requirements. Using various attributes to identify potential participants, SurveyMonkey identified about 1,500 management consultants who were likely to partake in the study, and the research studies focused on at least 218 participants.

SurveyMonkey sent out an electronic invitation letter to all potential participants who met the initial screening criteria to request their participation in the study (SurveyMonkey, 2013). The administrator from SurveyMonkey sent e-mails to all the participants with a link to assess the online survey study and a consent form. After the participants agreed to the consent form, they were granted permission to assess the study and took not more than ten minutes to finish the survey questionnaires. The link to the study was closed after a week to mark the end of the study so that no one could access the study afterward. SurveyMonkey, as a research company, has all the needed technology to help process the survey responses into SPSS format for further analysis. The returned survey responses will be stored in a secured location to provide the needed security and privacy. At the end of the retention period, the data will be backed up and protected with a password.

Increased Internet usage has enabled web surveys to have remarkable success, and they have been recognized as an effective way of conducting Internet research.

SurveyMonkey has gained much recognition as the leading Web-based research company and uses small incentives to its members to complete the survey studies. The services provided by SurveyMonkey enable the researcher to conveniently reach more people in different geographical locations; moreover, the online tools offer more flexibility to attain effective data analysis. In 2011, SurveyMonkey entered into partnership with TPG capital and was able to acquire three products of MarketTools as ZoomPanel, TrueSample, and SurveyMonkey. Additionally, SurveyMonkey has 1.7 million survey users; therefore, the three million panelist respondents and the needed technology to manage all responses make the company viable to provide research services to institutions.

Since 1999, SurveyMonkey, as a pioneer online survey and research company, has gained a positive reputation working with businesses, educational institutions, and nonprofits. SurveyMonkey has been used to work with educational institutions for research services, including Capella University in Minneapolis, Minnesota; Yale's Management School; the University of New Hampshire; Wharton School at University of Pennsylvania; University of Georgia; UNLV; Harvard Business School; Arizona State; Golden Gate University; Faqua School of Business at Duke; several campuses at California State and the University of California institutions; Baruch College; and City University of New York (SurveyMonkey, 2013). SurveyMonkey has provided assistance to both academic and organizational research studies that involve human participation (Barry, 2007; Berrios-Ortiz, 2012; Bobadilla, 2012; Brown, 2010; Etherton, 2012; Hooper-Boyd, 2012).

Data Analysis

SurveyMonkey has a unique platform that formats the responses of the participants to make the data ready to be exported to SPSS software for data analysis. The researcher eliminated all the incomplete and missing data. The software used for data analysis is the Microsoft Windows platform using IBM's SPSS version 21.0 analytical tool to analyze the data to provide scientific evidence to support the research questions and hypotheses derived for the study. The research study used descriptive statistics first of all to explain the demographic characteristics of the participants. The study used descriptive statistics including frequency table and other statistical measures to establish the relationship among the variables. The statistic techniques used include the correlation analysis with Pearson r correlation. Hinkle, Wiersma, and Jurs (1998) noted that the Pearson correlation coefficient matrix can ascertain the correlation between all possible pairs of variables. The Pearson correlation coefficients in any given instances range between -1

and +1, with –1 referring to a perfect negative correlation among the variables, +1 showing a perfect positive correlation among the variables, and 0 indicating that there is no correlation at all among the variables (Thorndike, 1978; Cooper and Schindler, 2008; Robeson, 2003; Swanson and Holton, 2005).

The multiple regression as a statistical analytic tool can establish at a significant level the selected independent variables to account for the proportion of the variance in a dependent variable, and this process can predict the importance of the independent variables. In this sense, the independent variables tend to be the predictor variables in the regression equation, which are assumed to be continuous variables. This researcher employed multiple regression analysis to determine the proportion of variance of the four independent variables (performance expectancy, effort expectancy, social influence, and facilitating conditions) to predict the importance of the dependent variable (behavioral intentions).

The independent variables in the regression analysis are important to determine the outcomes of the dependent variable. Cooper and Schindler (2008) explained the general statistical equation to evaluate the coefficients that predict the existing linear relationship for all variables that can be represented in the following formula:

$$\hat{Y} = \beta 0 + \beta 1 * X1 + \beta 1 * X2 + \beta 1 * X3 + \beta 1 * X4 + \epsilon$$

whereas

$\hat{Y}$ = a dependent variable (predicted value), recommended to accept VAT

$\beta 0$ = a constant value

The regression analysis was used to find out if several predictor variables (performance expectancy, effort expectancy, social influence, and facilitating conditions) were predicting a continuous dependent variable (behavioral intentions). According to Cooper and Schindler (2008), the main purpose of multiple regression analysis as a descriptive method is to develop a self-weighting equation not only to evaluate the contribution of other variables but also to evaluate the casual theories of variables. In line with the purpose of this study, multiple regression analysis helped to ascertain the relationship between the determinants of WAT acceptance among management consultants. The multiple regressions analysis is defined as multivariable techniques that possess the capability to ascertain the relationship between a dependent variable and multiple independent variables. The main objective of the research study is to explain the variance in the dependent variable with regards to the values of the independent variables.

Validity and Reliability

Venkatesh et al. (2003) determined the reliability of the UTAUT scale using the internal consistency alpha scores and established a value greater than 0.70 for the scale. Because this researcher looked at similar technologies that revolve around computers and electronic technologies and their application in the workplace, similar items were constructed but were tested for their own reliability. The survey instrument was adapted from an existing UTAUT survey instrument, which had been used numerous times by different researchers and has proved to be valid and reliable (Alawadhi and Morris, 2008; Carlsson et al., 2006; Venkatesh et al., 2003).

The instrument used in this research study for the purpose of data gathering was a self-administered online survey technique. In the area of technology adoption, many instruments have been developed with some of them designed for specific studies (Davis, 1989; Hebert and Benbasat, 1994; Moore and Benbasat, 1991; Venkatesh et al., 2003). This researcher made use of the similar construct items adapted from Venkatesh et al. (2003) after the authors granted permission for the researcher to change the word *system* to *WAT*. The scales of the UTUAT models have been proven to be valid and reliable in the original use and in other subsequent studies using the UTUAT model.

Furthermore, a field study was conducted with twenty-five business analysts who have both the needed qualifications and working knowledge of WAT to evaluate the instruments. The researcher used the professional social networking site LinkedIn as a platform to invite the participants to provide their opinion and feedback concerning the instruments. The participants received an invitation with a brief description of the study and the hyperlink to the survey study. The experts were expected to provide important feedback and recommendations to ascertain the reliability and the validity of the survey instrument.

Limitations

The type of the research study was cross-sectional, which made use of a convenient sample of management consultant in the United States. Venkatesh et al. (2003) explained the situation that technology expectations in both organizations and household are changing at a fast rate. Additionally, user perception and attitude with regard to a phenomenon can change over time, which makes a cross-sectional research study inadequate to provide profound explanation to behavioral intention to accept and use a given technology. However, to attain generalizability, it is recommended that this study be replicated using a longitudinal research methodology and, most importantly, with a different population or with the same population in a different geographical area.

An online survey research study is limited with regard to the issue of minimizing source of errors except for coverage, sampling error, and measurement error. The researcher has little control over the extraneous confounding variables that might have certain impact on data analysis and interpretation. Additionally, the statistical significance within survey design cannot be used to imply cause-and-effect relationships. Another limitation of the nonexperimental survey data is the point at which it is not capable of implying causality. Babbie (2007) argued that the limitations of standardized survey items are that they only represent the common denominator to assess experience and attitude. Furthermore, the nature of the surveys tends to be inflexible, which means any changes made to the existing instrument requires additional validation. There is also the probability that the participants might provide wrong information, which will not reflect the true situation under study.

Ethical Considerations

The research study conforms to all the ethical considerations as required by the Capella IRB. Cooper and Schindler (2008) suggested that all research procedures must be carefully outlined to protect the interest of the participants by first obtaining informed consent. Perlman (2006) summarized the *Belmont Report of 1979* in three categories as the respect for persons, beneficence, and justice. The researcher had to abstain from any conceivable unethical behavior and ensure that the participants understood their rights and responsibilities with regards to the research study. It was the responsibility of the researcher to secure the collected data and use it only for the intended purpose. The researcher provided the necessary measures to protect the confidentiality and privacy of participants.

The initial stage of recruiting the participants for the study included securing proper permission and authorization to use the services of SurveyMonkey. The researcher followed all the procedures outlined by the IRB to recruit the participants of the study by addressing all the ethical issues which included the participants signing the informed consent and making them understand the processes of the research study.

Creswell (2007) addressed the essence of maintaining confidentiality and protecting the participants' information. The identity of the participants was to remain anonymous and their data encrypted (Hatcher, 2005). The participants were not obligated to take part in the study, and they had the liberty to opt out if they wanted to. The researcher ensured that the study have no harm to the participants, as described by Leinsdorf (2007).

The participants involved only the individuals who had already expressed interest in becoming part of the SurveyMonkey survey panel. However, a consent form that indicated the purpose of the study, the benefits, and the risk involved was sent to the participants. As a research company, SurveyMonkey has all the necessary procedures to ensure that the participant's information is validated and verified from the existing database. After the participants submitted their responses, SurveyMonkey stored all the data in a secured database protected with passwords and firewalls to prevent data loss and any misuse of data. The researcher is the only individual who has access to the data, and the data were only to be used for the intended purpose of the study.

Conclusion

This chapter examined the research design and the methodology used to determine the relationship between the factors that influence management consultant's acceptance of WAT. The quantitative research methodology explored logical reasoning, numerical analysis, and statistical tools to provide objective analysis about management consultants' acceptance of WAT. Creswell (2009) explained that the use of quantitative methods enables researchers to make important references about a population with regards to a given phenomenon. The study used the target population sample of management consultants in the United States who are SurveyMonkey panelists. The data were analyzed using correlational analysis, multiple regression analysis, and descriptive and inferential statistics. Chapter 4 presents the actual data collected and the data analysis to support the research questions and the hypotheses.

CHAPTER 4

Results

The main objective of this study is to ascertain the determinants of management consultants' acceptance of WAT. This chapter furnishes the data collection procedures and the statistical analysis to establish the significant determinants of management consultants of WAT, to ascertain the relationship among the variables, and how the moderation factors affect the main variables. This chapter includes the description of the demographic characteristics of the survey participants and the administration of the survey through a research vendor, SurveyMonkey, to recruit the participants for the study. The second section of the study of this chapter explains the statistical analysis of the data collected from the survey study.

Description of the Population, Sample, and Sample Size Data Collection

The SurveyMonkey management team assigned a representative, who administered the survey study by sending electronically the initial invitation to the participants. The research questionnaires were sent to 410 prospects; 270 participants completed the survey. To select the participants that met the research criteria, the initial question was intended to determine if the participant was a management consultant or had any job requirement that included consulting services. The participants were presented with the general description of the study and the guidelines to participate in the survey. The participants needed to agree to the consent form before they were allowed to take part in the study for about ten minutes or less. The data were temporarily stored in the vendor's server and then uploaded to the researcher's computer for further data analysis. A copy of the raw data has been stored on a protected flash drive that will be kept for seven years.

Consulting Type

The participants who took the survey were either management consultants or any individual who performs management consulting services in various organizations. As already explained in Chapter 1, the internal consultants worked in their various organizations, and the external consultants are brought outside the organization to help finish an assigned task. As illustrated in Table 1, a majority of the participants were self- employed consultants (40.3 percent) managing their own consulting firms, followed by external consultants (18.8 percent) and full-time consultants (19.6 percent). The internal consultants were the least participants as (7.0 percent) and the part-time consultants.

Table 1 *Consulting Type*

Consulting Type	Frequency	Percentage	Cumulative Percentage
Internal Consultant	18	7.0 %	7.0 %
External Consultant	53	19.6 %	27 %
Self-employed	109	40.3 %	67 %
Part-time consultant	39	14.4 %	81 %
Full-time consultant	51	18.8 %	100 %
Total	270		

Gender

The data of the gender of the participants illustrated in Table 2 reveal that 63 percent of the participants were male and the 37 percent of the participants were female. Although the management consulting industry is dominated by men, the gender of the participants indicates close to 40 percent of women participation in this study.

Table 2 *Gender*

Gender	Frequency	Percentage	Cumulative Percentage
Female	100	37.0 %	37.0 %
Male	170	63.0 %	63.0 %
Total	270	100 %	100 %

Age

Previous IS studies considered age as an important moderator in determining behavioral intentions to accept a specific technology. The ages of the participants were categorized in four age groups, which are illustrated in Table 3. The modal age group was from forty to forty-nine years, which accounted for 37 percent of the participants, and 43 percent of the participants for were over fifty years. For the younger group, 8.8 percent were in the age group of eighteen to twenty-nine years and 11.1 percent in the age group of thirty to thirty-nine years.

Table 3 Age

Age	Frequency	Percentage	Cumulative Percentage
18-29	24	8.8 %	9 %
30-39	30	11.1 %	20 %
40-49	100	37.0 %	57 %
Over 50	116	42.9 %	100 %
Total	270	100 %	

Gender and Age Crosstabulation

The results of the gender and age crosstabulation indicates that most of the participants who were men were over fifty years and older; most of the participants who were women were also over fifty, as shown in Table 4. The next age group, from forty to forty-nine years, has twenty men and twenty women.

Table 4 *Age * Gender Crosstabulation*

| Age | Gender | | Total |
	Female	Male	
18–29	7	16	23
30–39	16	14	30
40–49	20	20	40
Over 50	57	120	177
Total	100	170	270

Education

The research studies included the level of education of the participants to provide the description of the level of education attained by the participants, and it was obvious that the management consultant industry required certain levels of education and years of practical experience in order to deliver value to the clients as trusted business advisors. The highest level of education for the participants was the graduate level at 49.2 percent, followed by 37.4 percent having at least a bachelor's degree (See Table 5).

Table 5 *Education*

Education	Frequency	Percentage	Cumulative Percentage
High School Diploma	29	10.7 %	11 %
Associate Degree	7	2.6 %	14 %
Bachelor Degree	101	37.4 %	51 %
Graduate Degree	133	49.2 %	100 %
Total	270	100 %	

Experience

Sun and Zhang (2006) noted that there seemed to be different variations in the measurement for experience in previous IS research studies. The research study explored computer experience as one of the three moderating factors and how it can predict the three determinants and behavioral intentions to accept WAT. The study focused on the number of years of experience working with computers. The majority of the participants (26.4

percent) have attained five to ten years of experience, which is then followed by 24.9 percent for less than five years of experience and then eleven to fifteen years (14.2 percent). The participants with more than twenty years of experience were 13.2 percent (See Table 6).

Table 6 *Experience*

Years of Experience	Frequency	Percentage	Cumulative Percentage
Less than 5 years	66	24.4 %	24.4 %
5-10 years	72	26.7 %	51.1 %
11-15 years	61	22.6 %	73.7 %
16-20 years	39	14.4 %	88.1 %
Over 20 years	32	11.9 %	100.0 %
Total	270	100.0 %	

Exploratory Data Analysis

Field Test

To ensure the validity of the instrument, a field study was completed using professional social networks like LinkedIn (LinkedIn, 2013) to invite business analysts with terminal degrees who have working knowledge of WAT. For the purpose of this study, the subject matter consisted of participants who had terminal or professional related qualifications and some knowledge about the new WAT technology. The invitation introduced the participants to a short description of the study, and the hyperlink to the survey was sent to twenty-five participants; eighteen of them fully completed the study.

The experts who participated in the survey provided important feedback to ascertain the reliability and the validity of the survey instrument. Based on the recommendations of Vogt (2007), the participants were asked to consider any possible inconsistencies between item questions of the survey instrument and the constructs that were to be ascertained. Moreover, the researcher requested that the experts evaluate all the instrument items to ensure that they are logic and consistent. The experts were to provide a broader view of the general understanding of the instrument. The researcher

informed the participants that any information collected during the validation of the instrument would not be used as part of the statistical analysis of the final study. The participants' assessments confirmed the results of the previous research studies that there were no inconsistencies found between all the items in the instrument and the constructs to be measured.

Reliability Analysis

The UTAUT survey instrument has been used in numerous studies and has been proven to be most reliable. Still, because the instrument was adapted to a specific technology like WAT, the researcher conducted a reliability analysis. The reliability analysis test involved twenty-three questions on the survey, which were based on a seven-point Likert scale reading disagree, moderately disagree, slightly disagree, neutral, slightly agree, moderately agree, and agree. The results of the reliability analysis indicated that all survey questions used in the study demonstrated associations with each unique construct's reliable relations to each question. Therefore, there was indication of a strong reliability measurement for all the factors used in this analysis. The accepted minimums prescribed to be 0.700 were all above that; the scale measured the desired constructs. This survey yielded values that met the minimum reliability score of 0.70 for most scientific research. Thus, they showed a strong reliability measurement for all the factors used in this analysis, coefficients that are comparable and consistent with past studies using UTAUT, as shown in Table 7.

Table 7 *Reliability Analysis*

Scale	Number of Items	Cronbach's Alpha
Performance Expectancy	4	.88
Effort Expectancy	4	.92
Social Influence	4	.92
Facilitating Condition	4	.73
Behavioral Intention	3	.95
All Items	23	

Summary of Results

Research Questions

For the purpose of the investigation, three research questions were originated for the study. The statistical tool used to probe these research questions was multiple linear regression analysis. The research questions were analyzed statistically as follows.

Research Question 1. What are the significant determinants of management consultants' acceptance of WAT?

With regards to the first question, a multiple regression was run to predict the dependent variable Behavioral Intention (BIscore) from the four independent variables, Performance Expectations

(PEscore), Effort Expectancy (EEscore), Social Influence (SIscore), and Facilitating Conditions (FIscore). The results indicated that the PEscore was not supported as a statistically significant variable to predict behavioral intentions to accept WAT (β = -.069, t = -1.259, p =.209). The remaining variables, EEscores (β = - .489, t = 9.400, p <.000.), SIscores (β = -.489, t = 9.400, p <.000,) and FCscores (β = .306 t = -5.746 p <.000), were significant determinants of management consultants' acceptance of WAT (see Table 8).

Table 8 *Coefficients[a]*

Model	Unstandardized Coefficients		Standardized Coefficients	t	Sig.
	B	Std. Error	Beta		
(Constant)	-1.096	.704		-1.556	.121
PEscore	-.057	.045	-.069	-1.259	.209
1 FCscore	.466	.050	.489	9.400	.000
EEscore	.278	.048	.306	5.746	.000
SIscore	.132	.040	.173	3.338	.001
(Constant)	-1.096	.704		-1.556	.121

Research Question 2. To what extent do the main UTAUT variables (i.e., performance expectancy, effort expectancy, social influence, and facilitating conditions) influence management consultants' intentions to accept WAT?

The multiple regression results indicate that the model was statistically significant: $F(4, 270)$ = 106.8, p < .000, R^2 = .617. The regression model was significant, as 62 percent of the variations of the behavioral intentions to accept WAT can be accounted for by the independent variables (see Table 9).

Kennedy K Amofa PhD.

Table 9 *Multiple Regression Model*

					Model Summary				
Model	R	R Square	Adjusted R Square	Std. Error of the Estimate	R Square Change	F Change	df1	Df2	Sig. F Change
1	.786[a]	.617	.612	2.59314	.617	106.908	4	265[a]	.000

a. Predictors: (Constant), SIscore, EEscore, FCscore, PEscore

Research Question 3. To what extent do the moderating factors (i.e., gender, age, and experience) predict the determinants (i.e., performance expectancy, effort expectancy, and social influence)?

For the third research question, three regression analyses were conducted to ascertain how the three moderating factors: age, gender, and experience, predict each of the three separate constructs of performance expectation, effort expectation, and social influence. The results of the first multiple regression to predict the EEscore with the moderating factors of age, gender, and experience indicated that, although the moderating factors of age, gender, and experience account for 12 percent of the variations in the main variable EEscore, the model was not supported .F=((3,270) (f 1.66) p=.177) (see Table 10).

Table 10 *First Multiple Regression*

						Change Statistics			
Model	R	R Square	Adjusted R Square	Std. Error of the Estimate	R Square Change	F Change	df1	df2	Sig. F Change
1	.135[a]	.018	.007	4.55597	.018	1.655	3	266[a]	.177

The results of the second multiple regression to predict the PEscore with the moderating factors of age, gender, and experience indicated that these moderating factors accounted for 35 percent of the variations in the main variable PEscore (f 4.360) p<.023) and was significant for predicting the PEscore, as indicated in Table 11.

Table 11 *Second Multiple Regressions*

				Model Summary					
Model	R	R Square	Adjusted R Square	Std. Error of the Estimate	Change Statistics				
					R Square Change	F Change	df1	df1	Sig. F Change
1	.187[a]	.035	.024	4.94737	.035	3.224	3	266[a]	.023

The third multiple regression to predict SIscore with the moderating factors of age, gender, and experience indicated that these moderating factors account for 47 percent of the variations in the main variable SIscore (f 270,4) p<.005.), and they were significant in predicting the SIscore, as indicated in Table 12.

Table 12 *Third Multiple Regression*

				Model Summary					
Model	R	R Square	Adjusted R Square	Std. Error of the Estimate	Change Statistics				
					R Square Change	F Change	df1	df2	Sig. F Change
1	.216[a]	.047	.036	5.32673	.047	4.360	3	266[a]	.005

The First Set Hypothesis Test

To test the first four hypotheses, a correlation analysis was conducted with the five variables (BIscore) as the dependent variable and the four independent variables as performance (PEscore), (EEscore), (SIscore), and (FIscore). To determine if there was any correlation between the five variables, a correlation analysis was performed with a Pearson r correlation, and there was a moderate positive correlation between the variables.

Hinkle, Wiersma, and Jurs (1998) explained that the Pearson correlation coefficient matrix can establish the correlation between all possible pairs of variables, and the Pearson correlation coefficients can range from –1 to +1, with –1 indicating a perfect negative correlation, +1 indicating a perfect positive correlation, and 0 indicating no correlation at all. Each Pearson correlation value in the table is a measure of the probability (p) that a reported correlation value would occur by chance across the 270 participant sample.

H_A1: Performance Expectancy will have a significant influence on affect behavioral intentions to accept WAT.

The results were statistically significant as the Pearson's r value is 0.466, indicating a positive relationship; therefore, H_A1 was supported. There was a significant, positive relationship between the PEscore and BIscore.

H_A2: Effort Expectancy will have a significant influence on behavioral intentions to accept WAT.

The results were statistically significant as the Pearson's r value at 0.604 indicates a positive relationship; therefore; H_A2 was supported. There was a significant, positive relationship between the EEscore and BIscore.

H_A3: Social Influence will have a significant influence on behavioral intentions to accept WAT.

The results were statistically significant as the Pearson's r value was 0.538, indicating a positive relationship; therefore, H_A3 was supported. There was a significant, positive relationship between SIscore and BIscore.

H_A4: *Facilitating Conditions will have a significant influence on behavioral intentions to accept WAT.*

The results were statistically significant, as the Pearson's r value was 0.737, indicating a positive relationship; therefore, H_A2 was supported. There was a significant, positive relationship between the FCscore and BIscore. As indicated in Table 13, the Pearson's *r* calculation revealed a moderate positive correlation between the variables.

Table 13 *Correlation Analysis*

Correlations

		PEscore	EEscore	SIscore	FCscore	BIscore
PEscore	Pearson correlation	1	.602**	.617**	.498**	.466**
	Sig. (2-tailed)		.000	.000	.000	.000
	N	270	270	270	270	270
EEscore	Pearson correlation	.602**	1	.451**	.609**	.640**
	Sig. (2-tailed)	.000		.000	.000	.000
	N	270	270	270	270	270
SIscore	Pearson correlation	.617**	.451**	1	.551**	.538**
	Sig. (2-tailed)	.000	.000		.000	.000
	N	270	270	270	270	270
FCscore	Pearson correlation	.498**	.609**	.551**	1	.737**
	Sig. (2-tailed)	.000	.000	.000		.000
	N	270	270	270	270	270
BIscore	Pearson correlation	.466**	.640**	.538**	.737**	1
	Sig. (2-tailed)	.000	.000	.000	.000	
	N	270	270	270	270	270

**Correlation is significant at the 0.01 level (2-tailed).

The Second Set Hypothesis Test

The multiple regression analysis process can predict the importance of the independent variables. To find out how the moderating factors of age, gender, and experience predict behavioral intention to accept WAT, a multiple regression analysis was run, and the result indicates that 41 percent of the variation can be accounted for by age, gender, and experience. The model was accepted with t =3.747 $p > .012$ (see Table 14).

Table 14 *Multiple Regression Analysis*

Model Summary

Model	R	R Square	Adjusted R Square	Std. Error of the Estimate	R Square Change	F Change	df1	Df2	Sig. F Change
1	.201ᵃ	.041	.030	4.09871	.041	3.747	3	266ᵃ	.012

H$_A$5: *Gender will have a significant influence on behavioral intentions to accept WAT.*

Gender was not supported as statistically significant as a moderating variable to predict behavioral intention to accept WAT ($\beta = .40, t = 9.91, p <.001. t = .686, p =.493$); therefore, HA5 was not supported.

H$_A$6: *Age will have a significant influence on behavioral intention to accept WAT.* Age was significant as a moderating variable to predict the behavioral intentions to accept WAT ($\beta = -230, t = -3.259, p <.001. t = .686, p <.001$). Therefore, H$_A$5 was supported, as shown in Table 15.

H$_A$7: *Experience will have a significant influence on behavioral intention to accept WAT.*

Experience was not supported as statistically significant as a moderating variable to predict behavioral intention to accept WAT (β = 0.72, t = -1.021, p =.308) .Therefore, H$_A$7 was not supported, as shown in Table 15.

Table 15 *Multiple Regression Analysis*

Coefficients[a]					
Model	Unstandardized Coefficients		Standardized Coefficients	t	Sig.
	B	Std. Error	Beta		
(Constant)	14.513	1.179		12.314	.000
q0003 Gender	.360	.525	.042	.686	.493
1 q0004 Age	-.740	.227	-.231	-3.259	.001
q0006 Experience	.208	.203	.072	1.021	.308

a. Dependent variable: BIscore, independent variables, b. age, c. gender, and d. experience

Conclusion

This chapter presented the demographic and the descriptive statistics of the participants. There was a reliability analysis to determine the validity and the reliability of the research instrument. The results of the correlation analysis indicated that all the constructs exhibited a positive relationship among all five variables: PEscore, EEscore, SIscore, FCscore, and BIscore. The multiple regression analysis was to determine if BIscore can be predicted by the four independent variables: PEscore, EEscore, SIscore, FCscore, and with the exception of EEscore, all the other three were significant. The multiple regression analysis regressions showed that the moderating factors of age, gender, and experience are significant in predicting PEscore and SIscore, but not EEscore. The results of the regression analysis using the moderating factors to predict Behavioral Intention to accept WAT also indicated that only age was significant, but gender and experience were not supported. The next chapter provides the full discussion of the research findings and their implications, together with the limitations of the study and future recommendations for research endeavors.

CHAPTER 5

Discussion, Implications, Recommendations

Introduction

To stay competitive in the global market, organizations continue to invest in their websites and web-embedded applications and software. These organizational situations mandate the use of WAT to effectively evaluate and manage all online activities to add value to organizational management and strategic operations. This research endeavor was intended to explain WAT acceptance by management consultants with the use of the UTAUT model. Prior research studies have confirmed the UTAUT model as a robust method to test new technology such as WAT (Wang et al., 2009). This chapter provides the summary of the research study and the discussion of the final results. The chapter concludes with the implications, limitations, and recommendations for future research.

Summary of the Study

The researcher used quantitative methods to make important inferences about management consultants' acceptance of WAT. The literature review in Chapter 2 underscored the previous IS research studies done using the UTAUT mode as a theoretical framework in quantitative research methodology (Moran, 2006; Pu-Li and

Kishore, 2006). The quantitative research methodology provided the necessary capabilities for exploring the logical reasoning, numerical analysis, and statistical tools to offer an objective analysis of WAT acceptance (Babbie, 2007).

The researcher employed the services of a research vendor, SurveyMonkey, to provide the platform for the online survey study. The SurveyMonkey administration helped to oversee the process of an electronic survey study with the provision of survey panelists and electronic delivery of the survey instruments to the participants. The duration of the study was five business days, and the data were collected for analysis and will be stored on a secure drive for seven years. The statistical analysis included correlation analysis to determine if there is any correlation among the variables. The next step was to ascertain with multiple regression analysis how the four independent variables predicted the dependent variables. The final stage was to use multiple regression analysis to determine how the three moderating factors of age, gender, and experience can predict the three independent variables of performance expectation, effort expectation, and social influence.

Discussion of Results

In this study, the researcher considered the relationship between the four independent variables, namely social norm, performance expectancy, and effort expectancy, facilitating condition and management consultants' behavioral intention to accept WAT. The study underscored the three moderators, namely age, gender, and experience, to predict the main independent variables. The study was grounded on the UTAUT model, which has been used extensively in research studies in the areas of behavioral intention for technology acceptance and usage.

The literature review in Chapter 2 established the scientific findings with previous studies in the field of study of technology adoption and usage. The early technology adoption models included the innovation diffusions theory, theory of reasoned action (Ajzen and Fishbein, 1975; Rogers 1983), the technology adoption model (Davis, 1975; Davis, 1989), which all supported the phenomenon that the behavioral intention to adopt a technology is considered as a good *predictor of actual usage*. The researcher equally reviewed the impact of normative beliefs and attitudes, users' past experiences, and other human factors on behavioral intention to accept technology and actual usage.

The study examines the original UTAUT model and how it has been used over the past decade. Recent research studies that used the constructs of the UTAUT model to determine technology acceptance and usage have confirmed the constructs successfully prove to be viable (Anderson et al., 2006; Chong, 2012; Sun and Zhang, 2006). The study focused on voluntary technology acceptance in organizational settings and involved the use of data gathered from 270 participants of the online survey panel of management consultants in the United States. The study presented the descriptive statistics of the population. The statistical methods used to analyze the data were correlation and multiple regression analysis.

Research Question 1: What are the significant determinants of management consultants' acceptance of WAT?

Regarding the first question, a multiple regression was conducted to predict the dependent variable, behavioral intention (BIscore) from the four independent variables (PEscore), (EEscore), (SIscore), and (FIscore). The results exhibited that PEscore was not supported as a statistically significant variable to predict the behavioral intentions to accept WAT (β = -.069, t = -1.259, p =.209).

The remaining variables EEscore (β = -.489, t = 9.400, p <.000.), SIscore (β = -.489, t = 9.400, p <.000,) and FCscore (β = .306 t = -

5.746 p <.000), were significant. This finding suggested that EEscore, FCscore, and SIscore are statistically significant predictors of management consultants' intention to accept WAT usage (see Table 10). In other words, the outcome of the research study showed that variance of management consultants' behavioral intentions can be explained by performance expectancy, social influence, and facilitating conditions, with the exception of effort expectation, which was not supported.

Research Question 2: To what extents do the main UTAUT variables (i.e., performance expectancy, effort expectancy, social influence, and facilitating conditions) influence management consultants' intentions to accept WAT?

With reference to Research Question 2, the multiple regression results illustrated that the model was statistically significant, F $(4, 270)$ = 106.8, p < .000, R^2 = .617. The regression model was statistically significant, for 62 percent of the variations of the behavioral intentions to accept WAT can be explained by the independent variables. To explain further, the four independent variables (PEscore), (EEscore), (SIscore), and (FIscore) account for the 62 percent of the variations in the dependent variable BIscore.

Research Question 3: To what extent do the moderating factors (i.e., gender, age, and, experience) predict the determinants (i.e., performance expectancy, effort expectancy, and social influence)?

Regarding Research Question 3, the results of the first multiple regression to predict EEscore with the moderating factors of age, gender, and experience indicated that although these moderating factors account for 12 percent of the variations in the main variable EEscore, the model was not supported: F= ((3,270) (f 1.66) F= ((3,270) (f 1.66) p=.177) (see Table 12). The results of the second multiple regression to predict PEscore with the moderating factors of age, gender, and experience indicated that these moderating factors account for 35 percent of the variations in the main variable PEscore (f 4.360) p<.023.), and they were statistically significant. The third multiple regression to predict SIscore with the moderating factors of age, gender, and experience indicated that these moderating factors account for 47 percent of the variations in the main variable SIscore. (f 270, 4) p<.005.), and they were significant in predicting SIscore, as indicated in Table 16.

The results of the correlation analysis indicated that all the constructs exhibited a positive relationship among all five variables: PEscore, EEscore, SIscore, FCscore, and BIscore. The results of the regression analysis using the moderating factors to predict behavioral intention to accept WAT also indicated that only age was significant, and gender, and experience were not supported (see Table 15).

For the purpose of the studies, seven hypotheses were proposed. The first four were to test if there are any correlations between the each of the indirect variable PEscore, EEscore, SIscore, FCscore, and the direct variable BIscore. All four hypotheses were supported (H_A1, H_A2, H_A3, H_A4). The next three hypotheses were to test how the three moderating factors of gender, age, and experience can predict behavioral intention to accept WAT, and only age was significant; (H_A6) as gender and experience (H_A5, H_A7) were not supported (see Table 16).

Table 16 *Summary of Hypothesis*

Hypothesis	Results	Accept/Reject Hypothesis
HA1	Pearson's r value is 0.602/ P<0.000	Accept
HA2	Pearson's r value is 0.617/ P<0.000	Accept
HA3	Pearson's r value is 0.466/ P<0.000	Accept
HA4	Pearson's r value is 0.493/ P<0.000	Accept
HA5	$P = .493$	Reject
HA6	$P<.001$	Accept
HA7	$P=.308$	Reject

The four indirect variables were performance expectation, effort expectation, social influence, and facilitation conditions, and the direct variable was behavioral intention. The moderating factors were age, gender, and experience. The following explains the constructs and the moderating factors of the research study as they relate to previous studies done, as explained in Chapter 2.

Performance Expectation

According to Venkateshet al. (2003), performance expectation can be defined as the extent to which an individual believes that utilizing a particular IS will enable him or her to realize benefits in job performance. As discussed in Chapter 2, Venkatesh et al. and previous researchers considered that performance expectancy should indicate the strongest predictor of IT intentional behavior and subsequent usage (Compeau and Higgins, 1995; Davis et al., 1989; Taylor and Todd, 1995). Several IS research studies provide substantial evidence that performance expectancy can predict user intention to use any given information system (Abushanab and

Pearson, 2007; Al-Awadhi and Morris, 2007; Al-Gahtani, Hubona, and Wang, 2007; Almutairi, 2008; Eckhardt et al., 2009; Oshlyansky et al., 2007; Sabah et al., 2009; Thamer and Bassam, 2013; Van Raaij and Schepers, 2008).

Therefore, the results of the research study indicated that management consultants perceived that the use of WAT might potentially enhance efficiency and productivity in the workplace environment. The findings indicated that performance expectation is a strong determinant of management consultants' behavioral intentions to accept WAT. The research findings are consistent with the original studies done by Venkatesh et al. (2003) and current research studies. The usefulness of WAT as perceived by management consultants is an important factor to consider for the successful implementation of WAT in an organizational IT infrastructure.

Effort Expectancy

Venkatesh et al. (2003) considered that effort expectancy is the extent of ease associated with the use of a given system. The original studies of Vankatesh **et al. proposed that effort expectancy tends to be a weak predictor in UTAUT with an R2 ranging from .08–.2, p<.05. On the contrary, research studies done in IS have confirmed that behavioral intention to use a given IS is determined by effort expectancy (Abushanab and Pearson, 2007; Eckhardt et al., 2009; Van Raaiji and Schepers, 2008; Thamer and Bassam, 2013). This researcher concluded that the construct effort expectancy was not a significance predictor of management consultants' behavioral intentions to accept WAT. The results showed that effort expectation as a determinant, which is defined as the degree of ease associated**

with WAT as perceived by management consultants, is not statistically significant.

Social Influence

Based on traditional norms and beliefs, individual behavioral expectations and attitudes are generally influenced by society. Venkatesh et al. (2003) explained that social influences tend to be a stronger factor to affect individual intentions to use new technology. Venkatesh et al. defined the construct social influence as the extent to which individuals perceive that important others think that they should use new technology.

Prior research studies proposed that social influence has a significant impact on individual behavioral intent to use a new technology as a result of attained satisfaction by conformity and identification (Moore and Benbasat, 1991; Venkatesh and Davis, 2000).

Venkatesh et al. (2003) and the preceding IS researchers explained that the intention to use an information system is determined by social influence (Abushanab and Pearson, 2007; Eckhardt et al., 2009; Lu et al., 2005). Similarly, the results of the research studies demonstrated that social influence, characterized by the awareness of management consultants' behavioral intentions to accept WAT, might be influenced by what the consultants believe other people think of them for using WAT, which was statistically significant. Social influence was significantly predictive of management consultants' behavioral intentions to use WAT and tended to impact positively on behavioral intentions to accept WAT.

Facilitating Conditions

Vankatesh et al. (2003) described facilitating conditions as how individual users identify the accessibility of organizational and technical resources to facilitate the use of a given system. Vankatesh et al. and current research studies have established that facilitating conditions are great predictors of IS users' behavior, which is more prevalent in mandatory use settings in which the individual user is obliged to utilize all available resources to be successful (Sykes et al., 2009). As discussed in Chapter 2, IS research studies provide empirical evidence that the user environment setting is imperative for IS usage success.

In the same vein, facilitating conditions are inclined to have a direct impact on intention and use of IS (Venkatesh et al., 2003). It was concluded in the findings that facilitating conditions are a significant predictor of behavioral intentions to accept WAT. The results supported previous IS research that successful implementation of WAT, like other new technologies in organizations, requires adequate technical resources and managerial support to create a favorable organizational environment for technology acceptance.

The Moderating Variables of Age, Gender, and Experience

In this study, the researcher considered the influences of three other variables: gender, age, and experience, on behavioral intentions to accept WAT. Voluntariness was excluded from the study as the fourth moderating factor. The research of Venkatesh et al. (2003) presented the essence of considering potential

moderating factors of user acceptance of technology. In this light, the study further proposed that the moderating factors of age, gender, and experience will significantly impact the behavioral intentions of WAT acceptance. Based on the results of the study, age was the only statistically significant determinant of WAT. Venkatesh et al.'s study identified age and experience to be significant in determining user behavioral intentions to accept a specific technology; moreover, the effect of experience on the determinant might decline with time.

Implications

Bacon's (2002) discussion of the constant changes of the computing environment and the available numerous online activities data make it essential to accept WAT to support global business initiatives and operations. The study demonstrated that management consultants will accept WAT because they have the behavioral intentions that WAT might enhance effective decision-making to increase productivity and efficiency. With the explosion of the Internet in multiple platforms, especially smartphones and other Internet technologies that include applications, the web is more essential than ever for global business operations (Roussos, Marsh, and Maglavera, 2005). The study using the UTAUT model has given increased understanding of the important drivers of WAT, the relationship among the determinants, and the moderating factors that will be a great resource for senior management teams to implement and sustain WAT in their various organizations.

The researcher equally noted that the management consultant industry can benefit from the use of the WAT to integrate online user behavior data, RSS feeds, and from other websites including social media for strategic decision and business planning for their clients. In the twenty-first century business environment, senior leadership encounters the challenge of the available voluminous data, which originate from diverse sources in both structured and unstructured forms that are sometimes in real time; thus, the use of WAT can help to generate informed and evidence-based decisions. The study implies that WAT will be accepted in organizations to provide all of these benefits depending on the implementation and how the technology will be sustained. The study provided important knowledge for web analytics service providers and other IT vendor companies about the important determinants of WAT acceptance and the relationships that are vital for successful implementation and sustaining WAT in organizations. The study on WAT acceptance is essential for understanding how online user behavior information can help website developers and website content managers make their sites more functional to meet potential user expectations. The results of this study could be used to predict potential user acceptance of WAT and measures for the development and implementation of IS policies in organizations.

From an academic stance, the study adds to IS literature on the technology acceptance model specifically to WAT acceptance. The study contributes to the IS literature in its exploration of the important determinants of WAT and their relationship in the context of business settings. From an organizational management perspective, this study will contribute to the body of literature on evidence-based management by identifying significant drivers of WAT. WAT is a valuable resource for enhancing change management to integrate the concept of analytics to strategic decision-making processes and other management operations.

This study adds to other studies in the management consulting industry that analyze the phenomenon of technological impacts on the industry. The online research vendor SurveyMonkey provided a unique research environment with higher standards and the needed technology to obtain survey participants across the United States. Similar to previous studies, the study **validated the UTAUT model using a new technology, WAT, and a different population consisting of management consultants.**

Limitations

The obvious limitation of this research undertaking was lack of time and enough resources as compared to longitudinal research studies. The research design was a cross- sectional survey study that collected online survey data at a single point in time and used convenience samples geographically limited to the United States. However, given that user perception and attitude about concepts change over time, to attain generalizability, there is a need for longitudinal research (Venkatesh et al., 2003). The main limitation of the nonexperimental survey data is that it does not have the capability of implying causality, and the statistical significance within survey design cannot be used to imply cause-and-effect relationships.

Online survey research studies are usually limited regarding the issue of minimizing sources of error, which includes coverage error, sampling error, and measurement error. The use of online survey techniques exhibits an issue in which the participants' responses are limited by their willingness to be honest on self-administered questionnaires and their ability to recollect information reliably. The other obvious limitation of the study peculiar with new technology like WAT, still in its infant stages, is that it can be considered to be a new technology with low capability awareness. There is a further likelihood that possible biases may be presented.

Finally, in the original study of the UTAUT, the authors used constructs in the context of organizational settings and their study included actual usage. This study uses a different technology and focuses on only behavioral intentions to accept WAT. There is a higher tendency to expect different results. Recent studies have developed new IS models and have combined them with existing models; it is recommended that the use of these models can extend understanding of WAT acceptance and usage.

Recommendations for Future Research

Regarding the numerous complex online data that organizations amass from varied sources, WAT provides a unique means to organize and utilize online data to support strategic management and operations. This study augments understanding of WAT acceptance by management consultants in the organizational context. Moreover, because the study was only a cross-sectional survey, it is recommended that to attain generalizability, the study needs to be replicated using a longitudinal research methodology across a given period of time. The new research study could also replicate the study in the same environment of the original UTAUT model research environment across different organizations. Future researchers need to explore WAT acceptance either using different populations or geographical locations, for this study was only done in the United States with a different population sample.

The research focuses on WAT acceptance; to fully understand WAT, it is recommended that future researcher examine the actual usage of WAT. The original UTAUT and recent models have originated new variables that could be used to extend understanding of WAT acceptance and usage. Furthermore, because the studies excluded certain moderating factors like voluntariness, new research studies might include them to extend comprehension of WAT acceptance. Additionally, future researchers could combine UTAUT model with other IS models to investigate WAT acceptance and usage in an organizational setting.

The final consideration is that the research studies that used an online survey technique with a self-reporting instrument could lead to potentially biased responses. Another area of interest that future researchers can be involved in can augment understanding of WAT acceptance and usage through both objective and subjective methodology. The research study that uses both objective and subjective methodology can provide more prospects to evaluate new technology acceptance and usage.

Conclusion

According to the research studies of Tan and Teo (1998), the Internet has become an integral part of organizational IT infrastructure and the hub for global business operations; therefore, the study of WAT acceptance is imperative for organizational management teams to integrate and effectively use online user behavior data to enhance their decisions and strategic planning. The main purpose of this study was to develop a model based on UTAUT premises to furnish empirical evidence to support management consultants' behavioral intentions to accept WAT. The study was to find the important determinants of WAT acceptance by management consultants and the significant relationships among the variables. The findings of the research studies showed that there is a positive correlation among the four determinants to ascertain management consultants' acceptance of WAT and performance expectation, social influence, and facilitating conditions were statistically significant. The study established that the four determinants accounted for 62 percent variation of management consultants' behavioral intentions to accept WAT. Generally, the results of this study significantly enhance theoretical and practical understanding of management consultants' acceptance of WAT and mainly provide the theoretical framework and recommendations for future research studies to probe into the phenomenon of WAT acceptance and usage.

References

Abushanab, E., and J. M. Pearson, J. M. (2007). Internet banking in Jordan: The unified theory of acceptance and use of technology (UTAUT) perspective. *Journal of Systems and Information Technology, 9*, 78–97.

Adam, D. A., Nelson, R. R., and Todd, P.A. (1992). Perceived usefulness, ease of use, and usage of information technology: A replication. *MIS Quarterly, 16*, 227–247.

Agarwal, R., and Prasad, J. (1997). The role of innovation characteristics and perceived voluntariness in the acceptance of information technologies. *Decision Sciences, 28*, 557–582.

Agarwal, R., and Venkatesh, V. (2002). Assessing a firm's web presence: A heuristic evaluation procedure for the measurement of usability. *Information Systems Research, 13*, 168–186.

Ajzen, I. (1991). The theory of planned behavior. *Organizational Behavior and Human Decision Processes, 50*, 179–211.

Ajzen, I., and Fishbein, M. (1980). *Understanding attitudes and predicting social behavior.* Englewood Cliffs, NJ: Prentice Hall.

Ajzen, I., and Madden, T. J. (1986). Prediction of goal-directed behavior: Attitudes, intentions, and perceived behavioral control. *Journal of Experimental Social Psychology, 22*, 453–474.

Ajzen, I., and Schifter, D. E. (1985). Intention, perceived control, and weight loss: An application of the theory of planned behavior. *Journal of Personality and Social Psychology, 49*, 843–851.

Al-Awadhi, S., and Morris, A. (2008, January). The Use of the UTAUT Model in the Adoption of E-government Services in Kuwait. In *Hawaii International Conference on System Sciences, Proceedings of the 41st Annual* (pp. 219–219). IEEE.

Albarracín, D., Johnson, B. T., Fishbein, M., and Mullerleile, P. (2001). Theories of reasoned action and planned behavior as models for condom use: A meta-analysis. *Psychological Bulletin, 127,* 142–161.

Al-Gahtani, S. S., Hubona, G. S., and Wang, J. (2007). Information technology (IT) in Saudi Arabia: Culture and the acceptance and use of IT. *Information and Management, 44*(8), 681–691.

Alwahaishi, S., and Snášel, V. (2013). Consumers' acceptance and use of information and communications technology: A UTAUT and flow based theoretical model. *Journal of Technology Management and Innovation, 8*(2), 61–73.

Amit, R., and Zott, C. (2001) Value creation in e-business. *Strategic Management Journal, 22,* 493–520.

Anand, V., Glick, W. H., and Manz, C. C. (2002). Thriving on the knowledge of outsiders: Tapping organizational social capital. *Academy of Management Executive, 16,* 87–101.

Anderson, J. E., Schwager, P. H., and Kerns, R. L. (2006). The drivers for acceptance of tablet PCs by faculty in a college of business. *Journal of Information Systems Education, 17,* 429–440.

Angehrn, A. (1997) Designing mature Internet business strategies: The ICDT model. *European Management Journal, 15,* 361–369.

Babbie, E. R., Halley, F., and Zaino, J. (2000). *Adventures in social research.* Sage, Thousand Oaks, CA.

Babbie, E. R., Halley, F., and Zaino, J. (2007). *Adventures in social research: data analysis using SPSS 14.0 and 15.0 for Windows.* Sage, Thousand Oaks, CA.

Bacon, J. (2002). Toward pervasive computing. *IEEE Pervasive Computing, 1*(2), 84.

Bagozzi, R., and Warshaw, P. (1992). Extrinsic and intrinsic motivation to use computers in the workplace. *Journal of Applied Social Psychology, 22,* 1111–1132.

Bandura, A. (1977). Self-efficacy: Toward a unifying theory of behavioral change. *Psychological Review, 84,* 191–215.

Bandura, A. (1986). *Social foundations of thought and action: A social cognitive theory.* Englewood Cliffs, NJ: Prentice Hall.

Bandyopadhyay, K., and Fraccastoro, K. A. (2007). The effect of culture on user acceptance of information technology. *Communications of AIS, 19,* 522–543.

Barry, A. E. (2007). *Examining college students' beliefs and behaviors regarding responsible alcohol consumption* (Doctoral dissertation). Retrieved from Dissertation Abstracts International-A. (AAT #3281028).

Bem, D. J., and Allen, A. (1974). On predicting some of the people some of the time: The search for cross-situational consistencies in behavior. *Psychological Review, 81,* 506–520.

Bem, S. L. (1981). The BSRI and gender schema theory: A reply to Spence and Helmreich. *Psychological Review, 88,* 369–371.

Berthon, P., Pitt, L., Ewing, M., and Carr, C. L. (2002). Potential research space in MIS: A framework for envisioning and evaluating research replication, extension, and generation. *Information Systems Research, 13*(4), 416–427.

Berrios-Ortiz, E. (2012). *Employee job embeddedness: A quantitative study of information technology personnel in the workplace.* (Doctoral dissertation). Retrieved from ProQuest Dissertations and Theses.

Birch, A., and Irvine, V. (2009). Preservice teachers' acceptance of ICT integration in the classroom: Applying the UTAUT model. *Educational Media International, 46,* 295–315.

Black, E. L. (2009). Web analytics: A picture of the academic library web site user. *Journal of Web Librarianship, 3*(1), 3–14.

Bobadilla, R. V. (2012). *Identifying metrics that private equity firms use to improve the quality of the products of organizations they acquire.* (Doctoral dissertation). Retrieved from ProQuest Dissertations and Theses.

Bose, R. (2009). Advanced analytics: Opportunities and challenges. *Industrial Management, 109,* 155–172.

Brightman, H., and Schneider, H. (1994). *Statistics for business problem solving* (2nd ed.). Cincinnati, OH: South-Western.

Brown, M.L. (2010). *Examining leadership and the laminated glass ceiling: Gender and leadership traits* (Doctoral dissertation). Retrieved from Dissertation Abstracts International-A (AAT #3399617).

Brown, S. A., Dennis, A. R., and Venkatesh, V. (2010). Predicting collaboration technology use: Integrating technology acceptance and collaboration research. *Journal of Management Information Systems, 27*(2), 9-53.

Brown, S. A., Massey, A. P., Montoya-Weiss, M. M., and Burkman, J. R. (2002). Do I really have to? User acceptance of mandated technology, *European Journal of Information Systems, 11,* 283–295.

Brown, S. A., Venkatesh, V., Kuruzovich, J., and Massey, A. P. (2008). Expectation confirmation: An examination of three competing models. *Organizational Behavior and Human Decision Processes, 105,* 52–66.

Calder, B. J., and Staw, B. M. (1975). Self-perception of intrinsic and extrinsic motivation. *Journal of Personality and Social Psychology, 31,* 599–605.

Callaway, S. K. (2011). Internet banking and performance. *American Journal of Business,* 26(1), 12–25.

Carlsson, C., Carlsson, J., Hyvonen, K., Puhakainen, J., and Waiden, P. (2006). Acceptance of mobile device/services: Searching for answers with the UTAUT. In Proceedings of the Hawaii International Conference on System Sciences, pp. 1–10.

Chan, F., Thong, J., Venkatesh, V., Brown, S., Hu, P., and Tam, K. (2010). Modeling citizen satisfaction with mandatory acceptance of an e-government technology. *Journal of the Association for Information Systems, 11*, 519.

Chang, I., Hwang, H., Hung, W., and Li, Y. (2006). Physicians' acceptance of pharmacokinetics-based clinical decision support systems. *Expert Systems with Applications, 33*, 296–303. doi:10.1016/j.eswa.2006.05.001.

Chatterjee, S., and Jana, S. (2004). Quantifying web-site visits using web statistics: An extended cybermetrics study. *Online Information Review, 28*(3), 191.

Chau, P. Y., and Hu, P. J. (2002). Examining a model of information technology acceptance by individual professionals: An exploratory study. *Journal of Management Information Systems, 18*(4), 191–230.

Chong, A. Y. (2012). Predicting m-commerce adoption determinants: A neural network approach. *Expert Systems with Applications, 40*(2), 523.

Cody-Allen, E., and Kishore, R. (2006). An extension of the UTAUT model with e-quality, trust, and satisfaction constructs. In *Proceedings of the 2006 ACM SIGMIS CPR conference on computer personnel research: Forty four years of computer personnel research: achievements, challenges and the future* (pp. 82–89). ACM.

Compeau, D. R. and Higgins, C. A. (1995). Computer self-efficacy: Development of a measure and initial test. *MIS Quarterly, 19*, 189–211.

Compeau, D., Higgins, C. A., and Huff, S. (1999). Social cognitive theory and individual reactions to computing technology: A longitudinal study. *MIS Quarterly*, 145–158.

Cooper, D. R., and Schindler, P. S. (2008). *Business Research Methods* (10th ed.). Boston, MA: McGraw-Hill.

Cornell, R. M., Eining, M. M., and Hu, P. J. (2011). The effects of process accountability on individuals' use of a familiar technology. *Journal of Information Systems, 25*(1), 109–128.

Crawford, M. E., and Fang, W. (2008). Measuring law library catalog web site usability: A web analytic approach. *Journal of Web Librarianship, 2*, 287–306.

Creswell, J. W. (2009). *Research design: Qualitative, quantitative, and mixed methods approaches* (3rd ed.). Thousand Oaks, CA: Sage.

Crowley, A. E., Spangenberg, E. R., and Hughes, K. R. (1992). Measuring the hedonic and utilitarian dimensions of attitudes toward product categories. *Marketing Letters, 3*, 239–249.

Curtis, M. B., and Payne, E. A. (2008). An examination of contextual factors and individual characteristics affecting technology implementation decisions in auditing. *International Journal of Accounting Information Systems, 9*(2), 104–121.

Czaja, S. J. and Sharit. J. (1998). Age differences in attitudes toward computers. *The Journals of Gerontology, 53*, 329–341.

Dambrot, F. H., Watkins-Malek, M. A., Silling, S. M., Marshall, R. S., and Garver, J. A. (1985). Correlates of sex differences in attitudes toward and involvement with computers. *Journal of Vocational Behavior, 27*(1), 71–86.

Davis, F. D. (1989). Perceived usefulness, perceived ease of use, and user acceptance of information technology. *MIS Quarterly, 13*, 319–340.

Davis, F., Bagozzi, R., and Warshaw, P. (1989). User acceptance of computer technology: A comparison of two theoretical models. *Management Science, 35,* 982–1002.

Deng, S. Y. Liu, and Y. Qi (2011) "An Empirical Study on Determinants of Web Based Question-Answer Services Adoption," *Online Information Review,* 35, 789–798,

Dillman, D. (2000). *Mail and Internet Surveys* (2nd ed.). New York, NY.

Dyck, J. L., and Smither, J. A. (1994). Age differences in computer anxiety: The role of computer experience, gender and education. *Journal of Educational Computing Research, 10,* 239–248.

Eckhardt, A., Laumer, S., and Weitzel, T. (2009). Who influences whom? Analyzing workplace referents' social influence on its acceptance and non-acceptance. *Journal of Information Technology, 24*(1), 11–24.

Ellis, R. D., and Allaire, J. (1999). Modeling computer interest in older adults: The role of age, education, computer knowledge, and computer anxiety. *Human Factors, 41,* 345–355.

Etherton, J. F., I. (2012). *Exploring voluntary turnover among IT professionals in defense contracting: A quantitative study.* Capella University). (Doctoral dissertation). Retrieved from ProQuest Dissertations and Theses.

Farney, T. A. (2011). Click analytics: Visualizing website use data. *Information Technology and Libraries, 30*(3), 141–148.

Festinger, L. (1957) *Theory of cognitive dissonance.* Stanford, CA: Stanford University Press.

Fillion, G., Braham, H., and Ekionea, J. B. (2010). Testing UTAUT on the use of EPR systems by middle managers and end-users of medium- to large-sized Canadian enterprises. *Allied Academies International Conference. Academy of Information and Management Sciences. Proceedings, 14*(2), 12–16.

Fishbein, M., and Ajzen, I. (1975). *Belief, Attitude, Intention, and Behavior: An Introduction to Theory and Research*, MA: Addison-Wesley.

Fincham, R. (1999). The consultant-client relationship: Critical perspectives on the management of change. *Journal of Management Studies, 36*, 335–352.

Foon, Y. S., and Fah, B. C. Y. (2011). Internet banking acceptance in Kuala Lumpur: An application of UTAUT model. *International Journal of Business and Management, 6*, 161.

Fowler, F. J. J. (2009). *Survey research methods, applied social research methods series, vol. 1* (4ᵗʰ ed.). Thousand Oaks, CA: Sage.

Gable, G. G. (1996). A multidimensional model of client success when engaging external consultants. *Management Science, 42*, 1175–1198.

Gefen, D., and Straub, D. (1997). Gender differences in the perception and use of e-mail: An extension to the technology acceptance model, *MIS Quarterly, 21,* 389–400.

Goldman, L. (2007). Web 2.0 brings web analytics 2.0. *DM Review, 17*(3), 28–28. Goldsborough, R. (2005). Gauging the success of your web site. *Diverse Issues in Higher Education, 21*(24), 37–37.

Goodhue, D. L., and Thompson, R. L. (1995). Task-technology fit and individual performance. *MIS Quarterly, 19*(2), 213–236.

Graubner, M., and Richter, A., (2003). Managing tomorrow's consulting firm. *Consulting to Management, 14*(3), 43.

Greiner, L. E., and Poulfelt, F. (2010). *Management consulting today and tomorrow: perspectives and advice from 27 leading world experts*. Routledge. NY: New York.

Hamm, S. (2009). Big blue goes into analysis. *Business Week, 4128*(2), 16.

Harrison, A. W., and Rainer, R., K. (1992). The Influence of Individual Differences on Skill in End-User Computing. *J. of Management Information Systems, 9*(1), 93– 112.

Harun, M. H. (2002). Integrating e-learning into the workplace. *The Internet and Higher Education, 4*, 301–310.

Hatcher, T. (2005). Research integrity: Ensuring trust in the academy. *Human Resource Development Quarterly, 16*(1), 1–6.

Heijden, H. (2004). User acceptance of hedonic information systems. *MIS Quarterly, 28*, 695–704.

Heldal, F., Sjovold, E., and Heldal, A. F. (2004). Success on the Internet: Optimizing relationships through the corporate site. *International Journal of Information Management, 24*(2), 115–129.

Hennington, A. H., and Janz, B. D. (2007). Information systems and health care XVI: Physician adoption of electronic medical records: Applying the UTAUT model in a healthcare context. *Communications of AIS, 19*, 60–80.

Hinkle, D. E., Wiersma, W., and Jurs, S. G. (1998). Correlation: A measure of relationship. *Applied statistics for the behavioral sciences, 4*, 105–131.

Hislop, D. (2002). The client role in consultancy relations during the appropriation of technological innovations. *Research Policy, 31*, 657–671.

Hong, K. K., and Kim, Y. G. (2002). The critical success factors for ERP implementation: An organizational fit perspective. *Information and Management, 40*(1), 25–40.

Hooper-Boyd, C. (2012). *Introducing leadership into the mix: An investigation of the relationship between personality characteristics and small business success.* (Doctoral dissertation). Retrieved form ProQuest Dissertations and Theses.

Hopkins, M. S. (2011). What's IT's role in analytics adoption. *MIT Sloan Management Review, 52*(3), 1.

Hsiao-Hui, H. (2012). The acceptance of Moodle: An empirical study based on UTAUT. *Creative Education, 3*(8), 44–46.

Hsiu-Fen, L. (2010). Applicability of the extended theory of planned behavior in predicting job seeker intentions to use job-search websites. *International Journal of Selection and Assessment*, *18*(1), 64–74.

Igbaria, M., Parasuraman, S., and Baroudi, J. J. (1996). A motivational model of microcomputer usage. *Journal of management information systems*, *13*(1), 127– 143.

Im, I., Hong, S., and Kang, M. S. (2011). An international comparison of technology acceptance testing the UTAUT model. *Information and Management, 48*(1), 1–8.

Ja-Chul, G., Fan, L., Suh, Y. H., and Sang-Chul, L. (2010). Comparing utilitarian and hedonic usefulness to user intention in multipurpose information systems. *CyberPsychology, Behavior and Social Networking*, *13*, 287–297.

Jay, G., and Willis, S. (1992). Influence of direct computer experience on older adults' attitude toward computers. *Journal of Gerontology, 47*, 250–256.

Karahanna, E., Straub, D. W., and Chervany, N. L. (1999). Information technology acceptance across time: A cross-sectional comparison of pre-acceptance and post- acceptance beliefs. *MIS Quarterly, 23*, 183–213.

Ke, W. L., and Wei, K. K. (2004) Successful e-government in Singapore: How did Singapore manage to get most of its public services deliverable online? Communications of the ACM, 47(6), 95–99.

Kelman, H. C. (1958) Compliance, identification, and internalization: Three processes of attitude change. *Journal of Conflict Resolution 2*(1), 51–60.

Kent, M. L., Carr, B. J., Husted, R. A., and Pop, R. A. (2011). Learning web analytics: A tool for strategic communication. *Public Relations Review, 37*, 536–543.

Kim, J., Park, J., and Koh, J. (2010). Determinants of continuous usage intention in web analytics services. *Electronic commerce research and applications, 9*(1), 61–72.

Kirchmeyer, C. (1997). Gender roles in a traditionally female occupation: A study of emergency, operating, intensive care, and psychiatric nurses. *Journal of Vocational Behavior, 50*(1), 78–95.

Kirchmeyer, C. (2002). Chance and stability in managers' gender roles. *Journal of Applied Psychology, 87*, 929–939.

Kitay, J., and Wright, C. (2003). Expertise and organizational boundaries: Varying roles of Australian management consultants. *Asia Pacific Business Review, 9*, 21–40.

Klaus, H., Rosemann, M., and Gable, G. G. (2000). What is ERP? *Information Systems Frontiers, 2*, 141–162.

Kohavi, R., Rothleder N. J, and Simoudis, E. (2002). Emerging trends in business analytics. *Association for Computing Machinery. Communications of the ACM, 45*(8), 45.

Koivimäki, T., Ristola, A., and Kesti, M. (2008). The perceptions towards mobile services: An empirical analysis of the role of use facilitators. *Personal and Ubiquitous Computing, 12*(1), 67–75.

Laguna, K., and Babcock, R. (1997). Computer anxiety in young and older adults. *Computers in Human Behavior, 13*, 317–326.

Layne, K., and Lee, J. (2001). Developing fully functional e-government: A four-stage model. *Government Information Quarterly, 18*(2), 122–136.

Lee, J., and Rho, M. J. (2013). Perception of influencing factors on acceptance of mobile health monitoring service: A comparison between users and non-users. *Healthcare Informatics Research, 19*(3), 167.

Lee, Y., Kozar, K. A., and Larsen, K. R. T. (2003). The technology acceptance model: Past, present, and future. *Communications of the Association for Information Systems, 12*, 752–780.

Leonard-Barton, D., and Deschamps, I. (1988). Management influence in the implementation of new technology. *Management Science, 34*, 1252–1265.

Leinsdorf, M. (2007). The ethical impact of business and organizational research: The forgotten methodological issue? *Electronic Journal of Business Research Methods, 5*(1), 21–28.

Lewis, C. C., Fretwell, C. E., Ryan, J., and Parham, J. B. (2013). Faculty use of established and emerging technologies in higher education: A unified theory of acceptance and use of technology perspective. *International Journal of Higher Education, 2(2),* 22–34.

Liberatore, M. J., and Luo, W. (2010). The analytics movement: Implications for operations research. *Interfaces, 40*, 313–324.

Lin, C., and Anol, B. (2008). Learning online social support: An investigation of network information technology based on UTAUT. *Cyberpsychology and Behavior, 11,* 268–272.

Lin, J. C. C., and Lu, H. (2000). Towards an understanding of the behavioral intention to use a Web site. *International Journal of Information Management, 20*, 197–208.

LinkedIn (2013). www.linkedin.com.

Loo, W. H., Yeow, P. H. P., and Chong, S. C. (2009). User acceptance of Malaysian government multipurpose smartcard applications. *Government Information Quarterly, 26*(2), 358–367.

Loraas, T. and Wolfe, C. J. (2006). Why wait? Modeling factors that influence the decision of when to learn a new use of technology. *Journal of Information Systems, 20*(2), 1.

Lynott, P. P., and McCandless, N. J. (2000). The impact of age vs. life experiences on the gender role attitudes of women in different cohorts. *Journal of Women and Aging, 12*(2), 5–21.

Marchewka, J. T., and Liu, C. (2007). An application of the UTAUT model for understanding student perceptions using course management software. *Communication of the IIMA, 7*(2), 93–104.

Marek, K. (2011). Chapter 1: Web analytics overview. *Library Technology Reports, 47*(5), 5–10.

Marrelli, A. F. (2004). The performance technologist's toolbox: Surveys. *Performance Improvement, 43*(10), 38–43.

Mathieson, K. (1991). Predicting user intentions: Comparing the technology acceptance model with the theory of planned behavior. *Information Systems Research, 2*, 171–191.

McLarty, R., and Robinson, T. (1998). The practice of consultancy and a professional development strategy. *Leadership and Organization Development Journal, 19*, 256.

Melville, N., Kraemer, K., and Gurbaxani, V. (2004). Information technology and organizational performance: An integrative model of it business value. *MIS Quarterly, 28*, 283–322.

Menon, T., and Pfeffer, J. (2003). Valuing internal vs. external knowledge: Explaining the preference for outsiders. *Management Science, 49*, 497–513.

Messineo, M., and DeOllos, I. Y. (2005). Are we assuming too much? Exploring students' perceptions of their computer competence. *College Teaching, 53*(2), 50–56.

Minishi-Majanja, M. K., and Dulle, F. W. (2011). The suitability of the unified theory of acceptance and use of technology (UTAUT) model in open access acceptance studies. *Information Development, 27*(1), 32–45.

Miranda, F. J., and Bañegil, T. M. (2004). Quantitative evaluation of commercial Web sites: An empirical study of Spanish firms. *International Journal of Information Management, 24*, 313–328.

Moran, M. J. (2006). *College student's acceptance of tablet personal computers: A modification of the unified theory of acceptance and use of technology model* (Doctoral dissertation). Retrieved form ProQuest, UMI Dissertations Publishing.

Moore, G. C., and Benbasat, I. (1991). Development of an instrument to measure the perceptions of adopting an information technology innovation. *Information Systems Research, 2*, 192–222.

Morris, M. G., and Venkatesh, V. (2000). Age differences in technology acceptance decisions: Implications for a changing workforce. *Personnel Psychology, 53*, 375– 403.

Motowidlo, S. J. (1982). Sex role orientation and behavior in a work setting. *Journal of Personality and Social Psychology, 42*, 935–945.

Nakata, C., Zhu, Z., and Kraimer, M. L. (2008). The complex contribution of information technology capability to business performance. *Journal of Managerial Issues, 20*, 485–506.

Nauck, D., Azvine B., and Ho, C. (2003). Intelligent business analytics -- A tool to build decision-support systems for eBusinesses. *BT Technology Journal, 21*(4), 65.

Nistor, N., Göğüş, A., and Lerche, T. (2013). Educational technology acceptance across national and professional cultures: An European study. *Educational Technology Research and Development, 61*(4), 733–749.

Nstase, P., and Stoica, D. (2010). A new business dimension – business analytics *Contabilitate Si Informatica De Gestiune, 9*, 603.

Ogle, J., A. (2010). Improving web site performance using commercially available analytical tools. *Clinical Orthopaedics and Related Research, 468*, 2604.

Omidvar, M. A., Mirabi, V. R., and Shokry, N. (2011). Analyzing the impact of visitors on page views with Google analytics. *International Journal of Web and Semantic Technology, 2*(1), 14–32.

Oshlyansky, L., Cairns, P., and Thimbleby, H. (2007, September). Validating the Unified Theory of Acceptance and Use of Technology (UTAUT) tool cross-culturally. In *Proceedings of the 21st British HCI Group Annual Conference on People and*

Computers: HCI ... but not as we know it-Volume 2 (pp. 83–86). British Computer Society.

Paul, A., and Erdelez, S. (2009). Web analytics in library practice: Exploration of issues. *Proceedings of the American Society for Information Science and Technology, 46*(1), 1–6.

Pelosi, M., Sandifer, T., and Sekaran, U. (2001). *Research and evaluation for business.* New York: Wiley.

Perlman, D. (2006). Putting the "Ethics" back into research ethics: A process for ethical reflection for human research protection. *Journal of Research Administration, 37*(1/2), 13–22.

Peterson, E. T. (2009). Competing on web analytics. *Journal of Direct, Data and Digital Marketing Practice, 10*, 214–222.

Phippen, A. (2004). An evaluative methodology for virtual communities using web analytics. *Campus - Wide Information Systems, 21*, 179–184.

Plaza, B. (2009). Monitoring web traffic source effectiveness with Google Analytics an experiment with time series. *Asib Proceedings, 61*, 474–482.

Plouffe, C. R., Hullan, J. S., and Vandenbosch, M. (2001). Research report: Richness versus parsimony in modeling technology acceptance decision: Understanding merchant acceptance of a smart card-based payment system. *Information Systems Research, 12*, 208–222.

Price, J. S., and Trainor, C. (2010). Digging into the data: Exposing the causes of resolver failure. *Library Technology Reports, 46*(7), 15–26, 2. ISSN: 00242586.

Pu-Li, J., and Kishore, R. (2006). How robust is the UTAUT instrument? A multigroup invariance analysis in the context of acceptance and use of online community weblog systems. Retrieved from http://portal.acm.org/poplogin.cfm7dl

Ranjit, B. (2009). Advanced analytics: Opportunities and challenges. *Industrial Management Data Systems, 109*, 155–172.

Rapoza, J. (2010). Web analytics: A new view. *InformationWeek, 1286*, HB2.

Reeser, P., and Hariharan, R. (2002). An analytic model of web servers in distributed computing environments. *Telecommunication Systems, 21*, 283–299.

Rhodes, S. R. (1983). Age-related differences in work attitudes and behavior: A review and conceptual analysis. *Psychological Bulletin, 93*, 328–367.

Rivera, M. A., and Rogers, E. M. (2004). Evaluating public sector innovation in networks: Extending the reach of the national cancer institute's Web-based health communication intervention research initiative. *The Innovation Journal: The Public Section Innovation Journal, 9*(3), 1–6.

Robeson, C. (2003). *Real world research* (2nd ed.). Malden, MA: Blackwell. Rogers, E. M. (1983). *Diffusion of innovations,* New York, NY: The Free Press.

Rogers, E. M. (1995). *Diffusion of innovations* (5th ed.). New York, NY: The Free Press.

Roussos, G., Marsh, A. J., and Maglavera, S. (2005). Enabling pervasive computing with smart phones. *IEEE Pervasive Computing, 4*(2), 20–27.

Rowe, R. (2008). Discussion of "An examination of contextual factors and individual characteristics affecting technology implementation decisions in auditing." *International Journal of Accounting Information Systems, 9*(2), 127–129.

Ryan, M. J. (1982). Behavioral intention formation: The interdependency of attitudinal and social-influence variables. *Journal of Consumer Research, 9*, 263–278.

San, M. H., and Ángel, H., (2012). Influence of the user's psychological factors on the online purchase intention in rural tourism: Integrating innovativeness to the UTAUT framework. *Tourism Management, 33*(2), 341–350.

Schaupp, L. C. (2010). Web site success: Antecedents of web site satisfaction and re-use. *Journal of Internet Commerce, 9*(1), 42–64.

Schein, E. H. (1996). Culture: The missing concept in organization studies. *Administrative Science Quarterly, 41*, 229.

Schepers, J., and Wetzels, M (2007) A meta-analysis of the technology acceptance model: Investigating subjective norm and moderation effects, *Information and Management, 44*(1), 90–103.

Sen, A., Dacin, P. A., and Pattichis, C. (2006). Current trends in web data analysis. *Communications of the ACM, 49*(11), 85–91.

Sharma, R., and Yetton, P. (2003). The contingent effects of management support and task interdependence on successful information systems implementation. *MIS Quarterly, 27*, 533–555.

Sheppard, B. H., Hartwick, S. B., and Warshaw, P. (1988). The theory of reasoned action: A meta-analysis of past research with recommendations for modifications and future research. *Journal of Consumer Research, 15*, 325–343.

Sheppard, L., Furnell, S., and Phippen, A. (2004). A practical evaluation of web analytics. Internet Research, 14, 284–293.

Spitler, V. K. (2005). Learning to use IT in the workplace: Mechanisms and masters. *Journal of Organizational and End User Computing, 17*(2), 1–25.

Straub, D., Keil, M., and Brenner, W. (1997). Testing the technology acceptance model across cultures: A three country study. *Information and Management, 33*, 1–11.

Stumpf, S. A. (1999). Phases of professional development in consulting. *Career Development International, 4*, 392.

Stumpf, S. A., and Tymon, W. G. (2001). Consultant or entrepreneur? Demystifying the "war for talent." *Career Development International, 6*(1), 48.

Sturdy, A. (1997). The consultancy process - an insecure business? *Journal of Management Studies, 34*, 389–413.

Sun, H., and Zhang, P. (2006). The role of moderating factors in user technology acceptance. *International Journal of Human-Computer Studies, 64*(2), 53–78.

SurveyMonkey. (2013). Retrieved from http://SurveyMonkey.com

Swanson, R. A. and Holton, E. F., (2005). *Research in organizations: Foundations and methods of inquiry.* Berrett-Koehler Store.

Sykes, T. A., Venkatesh, V., and Gosain, S. (2009) Model of acceptance with peer support: A social network perspective to understand individual-level system use, *MIS Quarterly, 33*, 371–393.

Szajna, B. (1996). Empirical Evaluation of the Revised Technology Acceptance Model. *Management Science* 42(1), 85–92.

Taiwo, A. A., and Downe, A. G. (2013). The theory of user acceptance and use of technology (UTAUT): A meta-analytic review of empirical findings. *Journal of Theoretical and Applied Information Technology, 49*(1), 48–58.

Tan, M., and Teo, T. S. H. (1998). Factors influencing the acceptance of the Internet. *International Journal of Electronic Commerce 2*(3), 5–18.

Tao, Z. (2011). Understanding mobile Internet continuance usage from the perspectives of UTAUT and flow. *Information Development, 27*(3), 207–218.

Taylor, S., and Todd, P. A. (1995). Understanding information technology usage: A test of competing models. *Information Systems Research, 6*, 144–176.

Thamer, A., A., and Bassam, M., A. (2013). Extended UTAUT to examine the acceptance of web based training system by public sector. *International Journal of Interactive Mobile Technologies, 7*(1), 4–9.

Thompson, R. L., Higgins, C. A., and Howell, J. M. (1991). Personal computing: Toward a conceptual model of utilization. *MIS Quarterly, 15*(1), 125–143.

Thompson, R. L., Higgins, C. A., and Howell, J. M. (1994). Influence of experience on personal computer utilization: Testing a conceptual model. *Journal of Management Information Systems, 11*, 167–187.

Thorndike, R. M. (1978). *Correlational procedures for research.* New York, NY: Gardner Press.

Treiblmaier, H. (2007). Web site analysis: A review and assessment of previous research. *Communications of AIS, 19*, 806–843.

Triandis, H. C. (1977). *Interpersonal behavior.* Monterey, CA: Brooke/Cole.

Turner, A. N. (1982). Consulting is more than giving advice. *Harvard Business Review, 60*(5), 120–129.

Tyran, C. K., and George, J. F. (1993). The implementation of expert systems: a survey of successful implementations. *ACM SIGMIS Database, 24*(1), 5–15.

Vallerand, R. J. (1997). Toward a hierarchical model of intrinsic and extrinsic motivation. In M. Zanna (Ed.), *Advances in experimental social psychology* (pp. 271–360). New York, NY: Academic Press.

Van Raaij, E. M., and Schepers, J. J. L. (2008). The acceptance and use of a virtual learning environment in China. *Computers and Education, 50*, 838–852.

Van Schaik, P. (2009). Unified theory of acceptance and use for websites used by students in higher education. *Journal of Educational Computing Research, 40*, 229–257.

Van Slyke, C., Belanger, F., and Communale, C. (2004). Adopting business-to consumer electronic commerce: The effects of trust and perceived innovation characteristics. *The Database for Advances in Information Systems, 35*(2), 32–49.

Venkatesh, V. and Morris, M. G. (2000). Why don't men ever stop to ask for directions? Gender, social influence and their role in technology acceptance and usage behavior. *MIS Quarterly, 24*(1), 115–140.

Venkatesh, V. (1999). Creation of favorable user perceptions: Exploring the role of intrinsic motivation, *MIS Quarterly, 23*, 239–260.

Venkatesh, V. (2000). Determinants of perceived ease of use: Integrating control, intrinsic motivation, and emotion into the technology acceptance model. *Information Systems Research, 11,* 342–365.

Venkatesh, V. (2006). Where to go from here? Thoughts on future directions for research on individual-level technology acceptance with a focus on decision- making, *Decision Sciences, 37,* 497–518.

Venkatesh, V., and Davis, F. D. (2000). A theoretical extension of the technology acceptance model: four longitudinal field studies. *Management Science, 46,* 186– 204.

Venkatesh, V., and Zhang, X. (2010). Unified theory of acceptance and use of technology: U.S. vs. China. *Journal of Global Information Technology Management, 13*(1), 5–27.

Venkatesh, V., Brown, S. A., Maruping, L. M., and Bala, H. (2008). Predicting different conceptualizations of system use: The competing roles of behavioral intention, facilitating conditions, and behavioral expectation, *MIS Quarterly, 32*, 483–502.

Venkatesh, V., Davis, F. D., and Morris, M. G. (2007). Dead or alive? The development, trajectory, and future of technology acceptance research, *Journal of the AIS, 8*, 267–286.

Venkatesh, V., Morris, M. G., and Ackerman, P. L. (2000). A longitudinal field investigation of gender differences in individual technology acceptance decision making processes. *Organizational Behavior and Human Decision Processes, 83*, 33–36.

Venkatesh, V., Morris, M. G., Davis, G. B., and Davis F. D. (2003). User acceptance of information technology: Toward a unified view. *MIS Quarterly, 27*, 425–478.

Venkatesh, V., Morris, M. G., Sykes, T. A., and Ackerman, P. L. (2004). Individual reactions to new technologies in the workplace: The role of gender as a psychological construct, *Journal of Applied Social Psychology*, 445–467.

Venkatesh, V., Speier, C., and Morris, M. G. (2002) User acceptance enablers in individual decision-making about technology: Toward an integrated model. *Decision Sciences, 33*, 297–316.

Verhoeven, J., Heerwegh, D., and De Wit, K. (2010). Information and communication technologies in the life of university freshmen: An analysis of change. *Computers and Education, 55*(1), 53–66.

Vishanth, W., Ramzi, E., Faris, A., Mahmud, A., S., and Yogesh, K. D. (2013). Examining the influence of intermediaries in facilitating e-government adoption: An empirical investigation. *International Journal of Information Management, 33*(5), 716.

Vogt, W. P. (2007). *Quantitative research methods for professionals.* Boston, MA: Pearson Education.

Wang, E. S. (2010). Internet usage purposes and gender differences in the effects of perceived utilitarian and hedonic value. *CyberPsychology, Behavior and Social Networking, 13*, 179–183.

Wang, Y. S., and Shih, Y. W. (2009). Why do people use information kiosks? A validation of the Unified Theory of Acceptance and Use of Technology, *Government Information Quarterly, 26*(1), 158–165.

Wang, Y., Wang, K., and Wu, M. (2009). Investigating the determinants of age and gender differences in the acceptance of mobile learning. *British Journal of Educational Technology, 40*(1), 92–118.

Weiss, A. (2004). Reason for ornery consultants (or why organizing consultants is like herding cats). *Consulting to Management, 15*(3), 44.

Weiss, H (2004). The art of consulting. *Consulting to Management, 15*(4), 14.

Welling, R., and White, L. (2006). Web site performance measurement: Promise and reality. *Managing Service Quality, 16*, 654–670.

West, D. M. (2004). E-government and the transformation of service delivery and citizen attitudes. *Public Administration Review,* 64(1), 15.

White, J., and Weatherall, A. (2000). A grounded theory analysis of older adults and information technology. *Educational Gerontology, 26*, 371–387.

Whitely, B., E. (1997). Gender differences in computer related attitudes and behavior: a meta-analysis. *Computers in Human Behavior, 13*(1), 1–22.

Wills, M., J., El-Gayar, O. F., and Bennett, D. (2008). Examining healthcare professionals' acceptance of electronic medical records using UTAUT. *Issues in Information Systems, 9*(2), 396–401.

Wilson, R. (2010). Using clickstream data to enhance business-to-business web site performance. *The Journal of Business and Industrial Marketing, 25*, 177–187.

Wittmann, A. (2009). InformationWeek analytics has a new home. *InformationWeek, 1241*, 94.

Wymer, S. A., and Regan, E. A. (2006). Factors influencing e-commerce acceptance and use by small and medium businesses. *Electronic Markets, 15*, 438–445.

Yu Shan, C., Tsai Fang, Y., Chin Feng, H., Chien, Y., and Chin Cheh, Y. (2011). The comparison of three major occupations for user acceptance of information technology: Applying the UTAUT model. *IBusiness, 3*(2), 147–158.

Zhang, Q., and Segall, R. S. (2008). Web mining: A survey of current research, techniques, and software. *International Journal of Information Technology and Decision Making, 7*, 683–720.

Zhou, T., Lu, Y., and Wang, B. (2010). Integrating TTF and UTAUT to explain mobile banking user acceptance. *Computers in Human Behavior, 26*, 760–767.

Zweig, D., and Webster, J. (2003). Personality as a moderator of monitoring acceptance. *Computers in Human Behavior, 19*(4), 479–493.

Appendix A.
Survey Instrument

Performance Expectancy

UTPE1: I would find the web analytics technology useful in my job.

UTPE2: Using the web analytics technology enables me to accomplish tasks more quickly.

UTPE3: Using the web analytics technology increases my productivity. UTPE4: If I use the web analytics technology, I will increase my chances of getting a raise

Effort Expectancy

UTEE1: My interaction with the web analytics technology would be clear and understandable.

UTEE2: It would be easy for me to become skillful at using the web analytics technology.

UTEE3: I would find the web analytics technology easy to use.

UTEE4: Learning to operate the web analytics technology is easy for me. Social influence

UTSN1: People who influence my behavior think that I should use the web analytics technology.

UTSN2: People who are important to me think that I should use the web analytics technology.

UTSF2: The senior management of this business has been helpful in the use of the web analytics technology.

UTSF4: In general, the organization has supported the use of the web analytics technology.

Facilitating conditions

UTBC2: I have the resources necessary to use the web analytics technology. UTBC3: I have the knowledge necessary to use the web analytics technology. UTBC1: The web analytics technology is not compatible with other web analytics technologies I use.

UTFC3: A specific person (or group) is available for assistance with web analytics technology difficulties.

Behavioral Intention to Use the WAT

UTBI1: I intend to use the web analytics technology in the next 3 months. UTBI2: I predict I would use the web analytics technology in the next 6 months. UTBI3: I plan to use the web analytics technology in the next 12 month

Note: The survey instrument was adapted with permission from "User Acceptance of Information Technology: Toward a Unified View," by V. Venkatesh, M. G. Morris, G. B. Davis, and F. D. Davis, 2003, *MIS Quarterly,* *27*(3), pp. 425–478. Copyright © 2003, Regents of the University of